FINDING YOUR

MORAL COMPASS

**Transformative Principles
to Guide You in Recovery and Life**

CRAIG NAKKEN

HAZELDEN

Hazelden
Center City, Minnesota 55012
hazelden.org

Library of Congress Cataloging-in-Publication Data
Nakken, Craig.
    Finding your moral compass : transformative principles to guide you in recovery
and life / Craig Nakken.
        p. cm.
    ISBN 978-1-59285-870-5
    1. Conduct of life. 2. Ethics. 3. Spiritual life. 4. Recovering addicts—
Conduct of life. I. Title.
    BJ1581.2.N36 2011
    170.87'4—dc23

                                                                    2011028552

Editor's note

Some names, details, and circumstances have been changed to protect the
privacy of those mentioned in this publication.

This publication is not intended as a substitute for the advice of health care
professionals.

Alcoholics Anonymous, AA, the Big Book, the *Grapevine, AA Grapevine,* and *GV*
are registered trademarks of Alcoholics Anonymous World Services, Inc.

16 15 14 13 12 11   1 2 3 4 5 6

Cover design by David Spohn
Interior design and typesetting by Percolator

To my wife, Jane

All the words in all the books, and there are none to describe how much I love and appreciate these decades together.

CONTENTS

Acknowledgments xi

Introduction: How I Came to Write This Book 1

PART I—THE THEORY

What Are Spiritual Principles? **11**

Positive Spiritual Principles 14
Negative Spiritual Principles 19
Spiritual Principles, Conscience, and Noise 21
Free Will 23
Principles before Personalities 26

Spiritual Principles and the Human Heart:
Our Drives for Pleasure, Power, and Meaning **29**

Instinct vs. Spirit 29
Choosing to Attach and Detach 32
Three Basic Drives: Pleasure, Power, and Meaning 33
    Our Drive for Pleasure 35
    Our Drive for Power 38
    Our Drive for Meaning 42
The Interplay of Meaning and Power 45
Combining Our Drives into Spiritual Harmony 46
Power Struggles vs. Integrity 47
Spiritual Principles and the Brain 48
Personal Value Systems 52

PART II—LIVING THE PRINCIPLES

Spiritual Growth on a Continuum:
41 Pairs of Spiritual Principles **57**

Judgmentalism—Openness 59
  Dave's Story

Unfairness—Fairness 64
  Heidi's Story

Refusal to Learn—Wisdom 68
  Aaron's Story

Willfulness—Willingness 73
  Daniel's Story

Perfectionism—Excellence 77
  Bertha's Story

Cynicism—Gratitude 82
  Jason's Story

Chaos—Discipline 85
  Hagar's Story

Separateness—Unity 89
  Becky's Story

Rugged Individualism—Relationship 93
  LuAnne's Story

Lies—Truth 97
  Spencer's Story

Inequality—Equality 102
  Canowicakte's Story

Apathy—Care 105
  Peter's Story

Shame — Guilt 109
   Leon's Story

Cowardice — Courage 114
   Mary and Jim's Story

Unmanaged Fear — Faith 118
   Marian's Story

Entitlement — Selflessness 122
   Mitchell's Story

Deceit — Integrity 126
   Val's Story

Unkindness — Grace 129
   Lotta's Story

Impatience — Patience 133
   Ted's Story

Self-Righteousness — Anonymity 137
   Xenia's Story

Disdain — Empathy 141
   Astrid's Story

Skepticism — Trust 144
   Helen's Story

Infidelity — Commitment 147
   Olivia's Story

Dishonor — Dignity 150
   Albert's Story

Greed — Charity 154
   Emilio's Story

Laziness—Perseverance 158
   Lewis's Story

Resistance—Acceptance 162
   Talma's Story

Resentment—Forgiveness 167
   Mikhail's Story

Control—Surrender 172
   Rashid's Story

Arrogance—Humility 177
   Herb's Story

Intolerance—Tolerance 181
   Luke's Story

Despair—Hope 186
   Gabrielle's Story

Indifference—Compassion 190
   Gladys and Hans's Story

Irresponsibility—Accountability 193
   Summer's Story

Hate—Love 197
   Paige's Story

Self-Centeredness—Service 201
   Ashley and Amy's Story

Disrespect—Respect 205
   Martin's Story

Ignorance—Awareness 208
   Annabelle's Story

Envy—Appreciation 212
   Barbara's Story

Unbridled Worry—Serenity 216
    Pauline's Story

Injustice—Justice 219
    Nelson's Story

Epilogue: Embracing Your Moral Development 223

APPENDICES

Appendix A: Positive and Negative
Spiritual Principles: Two Charts 228

Appendix B: Applying Positive Spiritual Principles
in Your Daily Life 230

Appendix C: Applying Positive Spiritual Principles
Worksheet 234

Appendix D: Using Positive Spiritual Principles
to Help with Anger 236

    Anger Worksheet: Applying Positive Spiritual
    Principles 237

Appendix E: Directing Our Energies toward
Positive Spiritual Principles through Language 239

Exercises 242

About the Author 243

ACKNOWLEDGMENTS

If I were to acknowledge and thank all the people who have added to this book, it would take a book in and of itself. There are my early teachers of values and morals; all my clients (who will remain anonymous), who teach me each time I have the privilege of sitting with them in their search for meaning; the people who helped save my life back in the early seventies; and the people who enrich it now.

But there are a few special folks I would like to thank.

First, my wife, Jane, a woman of good reputation and keeper of my heart. Sid Farrar of Hazelden, for his willingness to push me to make this book more personal. Scott Edelstein, whose talents took a 250-page sentence and helped shape it into the form it takes today. Gene and Cathy Snyder, dear friends whose support is always there. (Gene is a wonderful example of the positive Spiritual Principles described in this book.) Sarah Frey, my niece and goddaughter, for her willingness to read pages and offer ideas and support—but mainly for being the wonderful woman she is. L. G. Perrson, my Swedish friend and colleague, who has shared his world and the hospitality of his family (Gunvor, Calle, and Jennie)—and who, for more than twenty years, has given me a place, through the Granhult workshops, to explore and develop my ideas, including those in this book. Ove Rosengren, for the hours and hours of sharing with me his knowledge and ideas, as well as the generosity of his family (Lena and Elin). (Ove, a few more road trips and we'll have it all figured out!) Calle Fjellman, the man who started a dream in motion. The hundreds of Swedish counselors I've had the honor of learning from and laughing with. (They helped me discover that one can have many homes.) Michael, Helle, and Claire of Denmark, for the joy, the laughter, and the meals—but, most of all, for the friendship of these many years. To Plan A Treatment Programs in Copenhagen, for their support of my ideas. To the folks of Monday night meetings, where the ideas in this book get applied to matters of life and death. To my sister Kristin, for the love and safety we have always created in our relationship.

I hope this book can help others, as all of the above people, and thousands more, have helped me.

INTRODUCTION

HOW I CAME TO WRITE THIS BOOK

All moral conduct may be summed up in the rule:
Avoid evil and do good.

As a counselor for more than thirty-seven years, I've had a vantage point from which to watch the destructive and constructive forces inherent in all of us. I've watched good people become bad, but I've also witnessed the miracle of bad people becoming good. I was one of these.

This book was born out of a moment in my life some forty years ago; in 1970, I was a drug addict, a lost soul. The moment took place at night, for darkness and its shadows offered more solace than daylight. I had shot up a mixture of chemicals sold as cocaine mixed with a bit of heroin, but in reality I had no idea what traveled down the needle.

What I knew was that I was sick, having a bad reaction, sitting on a curb somewhere in the city, vomiting into the gutter. Images of my life, my family, what I had become, and the ugly things I had done haunted me. The angry, sad, drugged eyes of my mother, also an addict, haunted me. The look of defeat and disgust on the face of my father—a proud man, a veteran of World War II—haunted me as well. So did my sister's pleas for me to get help. All these images raced around endlessly in my head. I had become a source of pain and anguish for many, including myself.

After a while, I started wandering the streets in a manner befitting the lost soul I had become. I raged at the gods, *Why? Why is this happening to me? All I've ever wanted was just to be good!* I can't remember how long I walked the streets ranting, getting sick, and then ranting some more.

But eventually a voice came to me that brought comfort and an answer to my questions. *The reason you are this way is because you are evil.*

There was a comforting truth in this. The faces started to fade away, the voices quieted, and a peace came over me. Yes, this was what I had become; I was evil. I did evil things—hurt the people I loved, stole things, dealt drugs. I had betrayed everything and everyone who was important to me. It all made sense; I just needed to accept what I had become.

Over the next few months, my attitudes and behavior matched this new insight. Evil people do evil things. I let the anger inside me grow. I let my ever-increasing desire for alcohol and drugs grow, too, until I was high almost all the time. As the anger and the fears beneath it grew, I sought out symbols of power to help cover up the growing powerlessness inside. I bought and carried guns.

I remember a trip to Wisconsin, where I bought a machine gun and a handgun from a biker. I had sewn a pocket into the back of my jeans for my small-caliber Beretta. All of this made sense and seemed right to me.

But still, from time to time, late at night, the moral issue of what I had become would revisit me. I wasn't able to find lasting comfort in being evil. Something inside me rebelled against it. So, about once every three or four weeks, I would go to bed with razor blades, cutting at my wrist, hoping to drain the evil from inside me—or end the life that by now had become unbearable. During these nights I found out how hard it is to become a murderer, even if what is to die is oneself. This was my life.

At the time I was living with my sister. We had both been kicked out of my parents' home. She had just had a beautiful daughter, Jennifer. Through her, my Higher Power found a way to reach me.

One day, my sister asked if I would watch over Jennifer while she went to the basement to do some laundry. I said, "Sure," and downstairs she went. Soon after, Jennifer started to cry. The crying had nothing to do with me—she probably just wanted to be fed or changed—but her cries cut deep into me, and my shame started to flow. Like her tears that wouldn't stop, wave after wave of shame engulfed me.

A few minutes later, my sister found me in front of Jennifer's crib, on my knees, begging my three-month-old niece for forgiveness. Begging her to tell me what I had done to make her cry.

"What the hell is going on?" my sister asked.

In a moment of honesty—a spiritual moment born out of shame, desperation, and the tears of an innocent baby—I responded, "Kris, I think I have a drug problem."

She looked at me and said, "Welcome to the real world!"

We talked. She called her social worker and got some names and phone numbers of treatment centers in our area. I reached someone at Pharm House Crisis Center, and they directed me to call their treatment center. They sounded very nice and set up an intake interview for me early the next week.

At the interview, we sat on pillows spread about the floor. Three or four nice people with very long hair (my hair was short, for when dealing drugs it seemed best to look as normal as possible) asked me questions about my drug use, my lifestyle, and my past. I offered no denial, just honest answers. No one mentioned anything about actually *quitting* drugs. In fact, being naïve, I thought that a drug treatment program would teach me how to control and manage my drug use.

At the end of the interview, they all thought I would be a good fit for their program. The only problem was that they had a waiting list, so I'd have to wait a couple of weeks to get in. I said this would be no problem.

I went home feeling good that I would finally get my drug

use under control. About a week later, Pharm House called, and off to treatment I went.

I felt safe there — safe for the first time in years. All the people at the center were good, decent folks who laughed and joked with each other and with us residents. It was here that I learned that even though I was doing evil things, the real problem was that I had an illness.

I remember the night my counselor sat me down and explained the illness I suffered from.

The counselor told me all I had to do was take responsibility for whom I had become — and, oh yes, stop taking drugs and drinking alcohol, which had been made clear by then.

I didn't sleep at all that night. I just stared at the ceiling, thinking. *Maybe I can get well! Am I evil, or just sick, or some weird combination of both?*

I ran away the next day.

After a week I returned. I was there briefly before I ran away again.

I went to my sister's apartment. She answered the door with Jennifer in her arms. When I asked to come in, she said, "No, Craig, you don't live here anymore. It isn't safe for Jennifer or me to have someone like you living with us."

For the next couple of months, I lived with addict friends using drugs until I decided, *The hell with being addicted!* I would give treatment a chance. I went back to the treatment center, but they wouldn't let me back in, either. Instead, they directed me to their outpatient program.

I started to go to the Sunday night outpatient group at the Pharm House Crisis Center. I stopped drinking and doing drugs. I asked my parents if I could live with them; they were willing to let me as long as I stayed clean and sober.

I remember seeing my father cry just twice in his life. The first time was because of my mother's addiction. The second time was the day I met him at a bowling alley to tell him I had decided to go into treatment. This proud, tough man who had fought a war, had been part of the Army Air Forces, had been in two plane crashes, and had helped fly concentration camp survivors back to England for medical attention—this man cried when I told him I was going to drug treatment. Then he said, "Thank God! We thought you were dead." Then he gave me a good fatherly lecture about how I needed to listen to these people, *whoever* they were, and do *whatever* they told me to do. I remember thinking, *What's he crying about? I'm not that bad off.* I was five feet eleven and weighed 110 pounds.

It was in a carpeted room above Martha's Antiques that I started to learn how to be a human being instead of the predator I had become. Here I met drunks and junkies who would become angels to each other. We were a sorry lot, but we had style!

There was Glenice, a strong, tough North Minneapolis lady whose favorite thing was to lie around in her bathrobe smoking marijuana. The problem was that the seeds would pop and burn holes in one robe after another. She realized she had a serious drug problem during one of these moments, so she went out and bought fireproof robes.

Then there was Vern, a St. Paul junkie, who became my best friend. Just months before joining the group, he had charged into the same crisis center with gun in hand, thrown his dope-sick girlfriend over his shoulder, and run out with her.

There was Kristin, who became my sponsor when it was announced one evening that we all needed to get sponsors. Years later, Kristin introduced me to Jane, who is now my wife of thirty-plus years.

There was Mary, a tall, thin, quiet, but strong woman from the plains of Minnesota. She had been a teacher in New Mexico. She told stories of driving home at night after a day of drinking and drug use, and hallucinating herds of elephants on the road. She told herself, *I don't think elephants are native to*

New Mexico. It must be a hallucination. Then she would close her eyes and drive through the phantom herd.

Then there was our counselor and leader, John. He had waist-length hair and a stare that would send shivers up and down our spines. He was an interesting mix of care, dignity, integrity, and rage. He reminded me of those tough old sergeants in World War II movies: one moment swearing and kicking his soldiers' rear ends to get them out of their foxholes, the next moment wrapping his arms around one of his men, offering comfort and strength as every cell in the soldier's body shook with fear, sadness, and doubt.

This ragtag group of humanity saved my life and helped teach me how to be a human again. Collectively, we probably made one complete human among us all, but we were able to use that one to create many; to help each other face what we had become; and to remind each other that inside all of us were good, decent hearts. I have always loved these people, though we have gone our own ways and rarely see each other anymore.

Down the hall from the phone crisis room, we sat on the carpeted floor and "dealt with our shit." This was our Sunday night ritual year after year. The Crisis Center moved, but they gave us another carpeted room, and our ritual continued there.

Most of our growth happened outside of Sunday night group. We grew each other up while watching each other's backs. We cried together, screamed at each other, went to school and college together, nursed each other through illness and emotional struggles, and eventually turned into good people.

It was in these people's goodness, their comforting words, and their dignity that I could start to see and claim my own goodness. They taught me that good and evil have more to do with choice than anything else, that the greatest spiritual gift given to each of us is free will, and that addiction steals free will from us, while sobriety returns it.

Life was simple back then. Our task was to put together a day of sobriety, knowing that each day clean and sober was a gift, and a day's reprieve from the hell that waited not far away for all of us. Each day clean and sober held within it lessons and skills to be learned.

Eventually, John told us we needed to start going to Twelve Step groups, so we all started attending different self-help groups. It is here, in church basements, where everyone begins the evening by admitting guilt and being welcomed for it, that I've had the honor and privilege of watching countless people reclaim their lives.

Over time, the Pharm House group's influence started to fade, and the reflective and active atmosphere of Twelve Step meetings replaced it. Like creatures that left the seas and found a new existence on dry land, we left the carpeted floor of the crisis center and now sat in chairs. Instead of confronting and screaming at each other, we read to each other from books. We listened to each other put together and tell our own stories.

It was in these meetings that I first knowingly came in contact with the Spiritual Principles described in this book. We learned to place principles before personalities; we were to practice these principles in all our affairs. In order to do this, we had to know what these Spiritual Principles were. So we spent countless hours listening to people talk about how they brought Spiritual Principles to life through their actions and about the consequences they and others suffered when they failed to.

It was in these meeting rooms that I learned there is no failure in falling down, only in the refusal to get back up. That the simpler you keep your life, the richer and more complex it becomes. That discipline is not punishment, but a form of love. That good can come from bad. That bad can come from doing nothing. That living the right answer is far more important than knowing the right answer. That knowing can get in the way of doing. That joy can be as simple as a good (or bad) cup of coffee, a store-bought cookie, and the return of an old friend who's been out using. That we don't need to understand in order to do the next right thing. That the next right thing can be as simple as just showing up.

I've written this book to help others see and understand their relationships with Spiritual Principles in a deeper manner—and, I hope, with more clarity. I make no claim to be right. I have no desire to convince. I just wish to share some of my ideas, thoughts, and excitement about Spiritual Principles.

In this book, I share with you my truths, my understandings of what it means to be spiritual. Truth needs no soldiers, no champions of its cause, for it was here before we were, and it will be here long after we are gone. Truth is here to offer us strength. It doesn't need our strength; it just needs us to listen. It finds more pleasure in our humility than in our arrogance.

We are imperfect; in fact, our imperfections are our map home. This is the main message I've learned in my own recovery and in my years as a counselor. By accepting and moving through our imperfections, we get closer and closer to what we've needed all along—more love, and the fellowship of each other.

This book is divided into two parts: theory and practice. In Part I, I lay out my theory of positive and negative principles and how they play out in the heart, mind, and brain. Part II consists of forty-one descriptions of each pair of positive and negative spiritual principles with a story illustrating each one. The charts in Appendix A show forty-one positive Spiritual Principles and their forty-one negative counterparts. Each pair creates a continuum within which we move back and forth, depending on our spiritual condition. In Appendices B through D are directions and worksheets using these charts to put these principles into action in your daily life.

PART I

THE
THEORY

WHAT ARE SPIRITUAL PRINCIPLES?

THE COMPLEXITIES OF BEING HUMAN demand that we embrace some form of structure. This structure will help us organize our beliefs, and determine and declare what has value. The structure each of us chooses determines how we will live, what type of life we will have, and what type of person we will become.

But what will we organize around? What will provide direction for how we live?

For many, this structure comes from religion. For others, it comes from something similar but less formal: spirituality. Like religion, spirituality provides form for how we live.

In his book *The Spirituality of Imperfection*, Ernest Kurtz writes, "Spirituality is a lot like health. We all have health: we may have good or poor health, but it is something we can't avoid having. The same is true of spirituality; every human being is a spiritual being. The question is not whether we have spirituality but whether the spirituality we have is a negative one that leads to isolation and self-destruction or one that is more positive and life-giving."

Each one of us has a personal relationship with Spiritual Principles, whether we're conscious of it or not. Our relationship with these Principles is, like all relationships, fluid and ever changing.

Simply put, Spiritual Principles hold within them Spirit,

that larger life force (Spirit = breath) that is the focus of all religions and all expressions of spirituality. Knowingly or unknowingly, all humans operate from them. Spiritual Principles are the most basic components of human existence and interaction.

These Spiritual Principles aren't vague abstractions. Nor are they set in stone or imposed from above. Instead, they are manifestations of Spirit that animate us—either consciously, by choice, or unconsciously, by instinct. They are real, living psychological forces that energize and inform our actions and decisions, for good and for bad.

Spiritual Principles are the seeds; we are the soil.

There are two types of Spiritual Principles: positive Spiritual Principles and negative spiritual principles. Both types are transformative, but one has the ability to help us heal wounds and become better, more complete individuals; the other has the ability to bring out the worst of who we are and tear us into pieces. To create a clear distinction between the two in this book, I have capitalized Spiritual Principles when referring to the positive principles, and lowercased the term when referring to the negative ones.

Spiritual Principles, being of the Spirit, are intangible. We cannot point to dignity or disrespect as entities that exist in and of themselves, but we can see and experience them in the actions of others or ourselves. We cannot possess them, but they can possess us.

The more intimate our relationship with positive Spiritual Principles, the more good we are capable of bringing to the world and to our own lives. The more intimate our relationship with negative spiritual principles, the more fear and cynicism will color our perceptions and the way we deal with others and ourselves.

When we speak of spiritual development, we are talking about deepening our relationships with positive Spiritual

Principles and lessening our desire to use, organize around, or become dependent on negative spiritual principles.

Spiritual Principles are natural laws, each with its own attributes, consequences, and effects. One does not have to believe in a natural law—such as gravity—to come under its influence. We are bound to it. The same is true with both positive Spiritual Principles and negative spiritual principles. If we fill our heart and life with respect, compassion, dignity, and so forth, we will have a better spiritual life. If we operate from these principles' negative counterparts, we will experience spiritual decay.

Each positive Spiritual Principle has a specific purpose, and it directs or guides us in a unique way. Think of each one as a different medicine in a medicine cabinet, with its own specific purpose and healing function. Negative spiritual principles have specific purposes and functions as well—but they act as poisons rather than medicines.

Positive Spiritual Principles hold the Divine within them. By the Divine, I simply mean that collective sense of decency and morality that lives deep inside most of us. It is that part of us that wants to respect others and be respected by others. The Divine part of us is good and moral; it guides each of us in a loving and caring direction. We experience the Divine when we leave the comfort of our home to spend an evening sitting with a sick friend. We find it when we spend hours pounding nails at a local Habitat for Humanity home. The Divine is also found in the collective conscience of people gathering in self-help groups to heal present and past wounds.

The Divine always works to heal rather than to harm. It pushes us to become better than we presently are. Because it requires us to change, however, we often resist its call.

Negative spiritual principles reflect the instinctual, animal side of our being. They focus not on serving, but on acquiring; not on community, but on putting ourselves first. The nature of instinct is to make sure we get what we want and feel we deserve, to feed our egos. This part of us wants an illusory assurance of safety and fairness, and it wants to blame someone when things don't go our way. When we are sure that the world is unfair, that everyone is out to get us, or that the rightness of our cause is obvious, we've most likely turned to negative spiritual principles for the false comfort they offer. If we regularly operate from these negative spiritual principles, we deprive our spirits, minds, and intuitions of vital nourishment.

Our relationship with Spiritual Principles largely dictates how we perceive the world. Positive Spiritual Principles foster interconnectedness among the different parts, helping us see and make sense of the big picture. Negative spiritual principles focus on the parts and how these parts affect ourselves. When we operate from negative spiritual principles, we tend to oversimplify problems and solutions, and then back up these oversimplifications with arrogance and noise.

The following two charts show symbols for the forty-one positive Spiritual Principles and their corresponding negative principles. I created these charts and symbols to use in the applications of these principles in exercises that you'll find in Appendices B through D; you will also find these in charts in Appendix A for easy reference when you do the exercises.

Positive Spiritual Principles

Positive Spiritual Principles represent the best of what it means to be human. The more we incorporate their intentions into our actions and lives, the more access we have to their enormous strengthening, regenerative, and transformative properties.

There is a collective dimension to positive Spiritual Principles. All positive Spiritual Principles encourage and support

POSITIVE SPIRITUAL PRINCIPLES

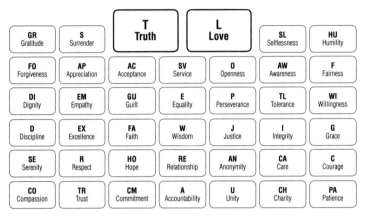

GR Gratitude	S Surrender	T Truth	L Love	SL Selflessness	HU Humility
FO Forgiveness	AP Appreciation	AC Acceptance	SV Service	O Openness	AW Awareness	F Fairness
DI Dignity	EM Empathy	GU Guilt	E Equality	P Perseverance	TL Tolerance	WI Willingness
D Discipline	EX Excellence	FA Faith	W Wisdom	J Justice	I Integrity	G Grace
SE Serenity	R Respect	HO Hope	RE Relationship	AN Anonymity	CA Care	C Courage
CO Compassion	TR Trust	CM Commitment	A Accountability	U Unity	CH Charity	PA Patience

Positive Spiritual Principles, being of the Divine, release ethical power and have the ability to heal wounds when placed into action. It is in how we bring them together that our value system gets created.

NEGATIVE SPIRITUAL PRINCIPLES

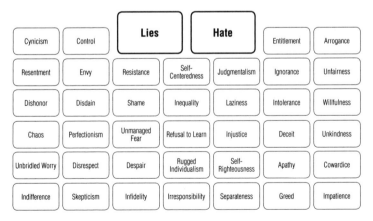

Cynicism	Control	Lies	Hate	Entitlement	Arrogance
Resentment	Envy	Resistance	Self-Centeredness	Judgmentalism	Ignorance	Unfairness
Dishonor	Disdain	Shame	Inequality	Laziness	Intolerance	Willfulness
Chaos	Perfectionism	Unmanaged Fear	Refusal to Learn	Injustice	Deceit	Unkindness
Unbridled Worry	Disrespect	Despair	Rugged Individualism	Self-Righteousness	Apathy	Cowardice
Indifference	Skepticism	Infidelity	Irresponsibility	Separateness	Greed	Impatience

each other; I think of them as family members of the Divine. For example, a week ago my nephew, his family, my wife, and I worked with others at a project called Feed My Starving Children. For a couple of hours, we put together meals for children and their parents who, because of conditions beyond their control, are in need of food. My nephew had volunteered as part of his confirmation commitment. We were with him because we love him and wanted to support his efforts to be a good young man. Two other volunteer groups were children helping out as part of birthday parties. For those two hours, many positive Spiritual Principles—selflessness, compassion, unity, service, and more—came together to help others. All of us were connected by a shared task and shared intentions. Plus, we had fun.

Positive Spiritual Principles remind us that there is a collective humanity that we are part of and need to sacrifice for. When we embrace and act from positive Spiritual Principles, we move beyond our self-centeredness, our desires, and our instinctive indifference to others. We become better at caring for and about the life we have been given.

Differences frighten our instinctual side, but they make our spiritual side curious. Instinct wants us to stay on the surface, to think one-dimensionally, to see differences more than commonalities, to stay separate from others. But positive Spiritual Principles, because of their depth, enable us to think and act three-dimensionally. Guided by these Principles, we learn how to weave pleasure, power, and meaning into a harmonic entity.

Positive Spiritual Principles have a unique energy, a unique rhythm. By acting in accordance with their essence, we release this spiritual energy, and for a brief time, it enriches our spirit.

When we practice a positive Spiritual Principle, we are called not only to act in accordance with it, but to work to *become* the Principle. This is the transformation we need to seek.

Surrender to a positive Spiritual Principle can occur two ways: through attitude and through action. We are called not just to act respectfully, but to *become* respectable; not just to act with dignity, but to *become* dignified. We work to be transformed into the essence of each Principle.

Becoming dignified doesn't occur through one action; this transformation only occurs through many actions that have dignity at their cores. Those two hours of putting meals together didn't make me a dignified person—but similar actions, taken regularly over a lifetime, may.

Unlike human beings, who are half animal, half Spirit, positive Spiritual Principles are pure Spirit. Their catch is that they need relationship in order to be brought to life. Morality only takes place within the context of relationships. We partner with positive Spiritual Principles; they need us to carry them into the light.

Through our actions and relationships, we activate and release the healing elements embedded within positive Spiritual Principles. Thus we become active representatives and representations of these Principles; thus we become moral beings.

The main by-products of practicing positive Spiritual Principles are more intimacy and love in our relationships with others, ourselves, and the Divine. But we will not know the full power and healing ability of these positive Spiritual Principles until we are able to achieve long-term relationships with them. For example, someone once told me about his relationship with his best friend: "Now that we're both in our sixties, I really see what a decent man Paul is. I've always liked him and thought highly of him, but it's only now, looking back at the layers and layers of good things he has done, the way he has carried himself, that I can see what a truly good man he is." The longer and closer our relationships with positive Spiritual Principles become, the more we see how important they are and how much good they can do for the world and for us. And in practice, it is mainly in long-term relationships with positive Spiritual Principles that transformation occurs.

We cannot possess any positive Spiritual Principle. Trying to do so is like grasping water: The tighter we grab it, the quicker it rushes through our fingers and back from where it came. We must cup it, hold it gently, and then drink of it, so it can nourish and refresh us before it slips through our fingers and is gone. Then we must seek it again. (This is another beauty of positive Spiritual Principles: We must rediscover them over and over throughout our lives, experiencing them like the awesome beauty of one sunset after another.)

Our instinct fears vulnerability. But only through vulnerability can we be transformed by positive Spiritual Principles. The ethical power embedded within positive Spiritual Principles transforms instinctual fears into deeper relationships with others, the Divine, our communities, and ourselves. As we surrender the energies of our fears, and surrender ourselves to transformation, a new individual starts to emerge— a person with ethical strength and an increased capacity to be vulnerable.

Spiritual growth is much like learning math: Once you master algebra, you can solve a wide range of algebraic problems. But the next challenge and task is then to struggle with and master geometry. Then you can solve a wide range of geometric problems. Once you've mastered geometry, the next challenge is to struggle with and master calculus—and so on. The same holds true for spiritual growth: The deeper your relationships with positive Spiritual Principles are, the more able you are to handle and struggle with the complex problems life presents. You will also find more meaning within life's struggle, while knowing there is always more to be learned.

Positive Spiritual Principles are also challenges. They challenge us to become better than we are now. They challenge us to serve rather than to find others to serve us. They challenge us to follow them and to live up to their standards in everything we do, in every moment of our lives.

We'll need to regularly stop and reflect on our relationship with each of these Principles and our relationship with them collectively. Many people do a daily inventory of how they are conducting themselves. Many go on retreats, often in places that have special meaning for them, to reflect on how they are conducting themselves.

Negative Spiritual Principles

Negative spiritual principles keep us tied to and trusting in our instinctual, animal side. Collectively, they become our puffed-up ego pounding its chest and demanding that others yield to its desires. We often experience these principles as illusions of safety and comfort.

Here's an example: Someone states something as a fact, but we know or believe it to be false. We feel superior; we see this person as dumb; we think, *What a fool he is to believe that!* At that moment, we find some comfort, some internal joy, for we have stepped into the negative spiritual principles of self-righteousness and arrogance, which create powerful sensations for us. Instinct balks at investigation; it doesn't seek truth; it seeks control. Nevertheless, it has the power to comfort our frightened egos.

A common characteristic of negative spiritual principles is their ability to create a false, illusory sense of control. This is their siren song, and why (in part) they're so attractive.

Our attraction to negative spiritual principles is also based on fear, uncertainty, a feeling of powerlessness, or a painful emotion we don't want to feel. Our instinctual side hopes to distance us from these emotions through a sense of control. Yet we humans can genuinely control very little; we can influence, but not control. Positive Spiritual Principles help us understand and accept this. Yet our instinctual side believes in, dreams of, and tries to wield unlimited control over people and situations. This is spiritual immaturity.

Negative spiritual principles do not offer us solutions— only the illusion of solutions. We make decisions but find no genuine solutions.

When operating from negative spiritual principles, we seek to dominate others or our problems rather than learn from them. Domination creates a momentary illusion of a solution, but it is a house of cards that will collapse in even the slightest breeze.

Instinct and negative spiritual principles reduce us to merely reacting to what is happening around us. Here's a common example: Our teenager hasn't come home yet, and it's an hour after her curfew. We're afraid. *Was there an accident? Is she out getting drunk? Why hasn't she called?* When she walks in a few minutes later, we look at our watch and yell at her for being irresponsible and inconsiderate. We tell her to go to her room and that she's grounded for a month.

Our fear for our child's safety has triggered our instinctual desire to control things. So we try to control the situation and our child—and, in the process, we embody the negative spiritual principles of judgmentalism and unkindness. In order to avoid the pain of our own guilt, we may then rely on another negative spiritual principle: shame. We say to ourselves, *If my child would just act right, I wouldn't have to scream at her.* But reactions are not solutions; they are just our instinctual attempts to deal with our fear and emotional pain. Negative spiritual principles thus disrupt our relationships with others, our communities, the Divine, and ourselves.

Like positive Spiritual Principles, negative spiritual principles have transformative powers. If we cling to or habitually rely on negative spiritual principles, they become character defects.

Eventually, we may turn into angry cynics who are afraid of anything that challenges us to give up our negativity. We may then slip into serious spiritual decay, developing a hardened heart and living a life of bitterness and broken relationships.

Knowing, naming, and identifying negative spiritual principles can help us become more attuned to them when we encounter them, both in others and (especially) in ourselves. For example, when we feel cynical and realize we are about to make a cynical remark, we can catch and recenter ourselves, using gratitude as our guiding positive Spiritual Principle.

Spiritual Principles, Conscience, and Noise

The collective voice of positive Spiritual Principles is called our conscience—that inner sense of what is good and what impels us toward helpful actions. Conscience is there to help us master and redirect our fears, anger, and sadness. If we have no relationship with positive Spiritual Principles, living only by negative ones, we'll have no conscience. If we have underdeveloped relationships with positive Spiritual Principles, we will have an underdeveloped conscience.

Conscience is the voice of the Divine, speaking through our relationships with positive Spiritual Principles. It is a creative force seeking to create new perspectives and open us to new worlds.

In a class I taught some years ago, I listened to a man in a nice sport jacket and tie talk about how, a year earlier, he had been living in a cardboard box behind a bar. Each day he would wake up with the shakes. The owner of the bar would let him clean up the bar; in return, this man would get the booze he needed to keep the DTs away.

One day he walked into the Salvation Army to get a meal, as he had many times before, and as he sat down, a woman sat down beside him. They ate quietly. When she was done, she stood up. But before she walked away, she looked down at him, and their eyes met. In her eyes he saw pure love. She said to him, "It's time for this to end. It's time for you to return home. Go talk to that man and he will help you. Do what he says." She pointed to one of the counselors.

He went to the counselor. They talked, and he moved in to the Salvation Army and began its addiction treatment program. Since then, he had stayed sober, working and living at the center. In the year since he encountered that woman, he never saw her again.

He explained to the class, "I had lost my conscience, my hope, my sense of purpose. That day, in that woman's eyes, I found a way out of that cardboard box and back to life. I had to become the care and love that I had seen in them. She was my conscience when I had none."

Was she real, or part of one of his many drunken hallucinations? Either way, in this man's eyes, it was conscience inviting him home. And he listened.

We need a conscience. It protects us from losing our sense of values and becoming distracted by the material things that surround us. It keeps us vital and spiritually alive. It guides us in our search for meaning. It is one of the things that make us human. In the words of Viktor Frankl, "Conscience could be defined as the intuitive capacity of man to find out the meaning of a situation."

Conscience usually speaks a quiet and subtle voice. Thus we must seek quiet places, or learn to quiet ourselves, or do both in order to hear its guidance.

Negative spiritual principles create noise, and noise makes it very hard—and often almost impossible—to sort out what positive Spiritual Principles call us to do. Noise can, and often does, drown out the voice of conscience. We may then respond instinctually, reacting to emotions such as fear and sadness by seeking comfort, illusory safety, or even revenge. Reflections get replaced by opinions. Investigation gets replaced with contempt.

Sadly, negative spiritual principles are often promoted—and encouraged—as entertainment or truth. A good friend was invited onto a national daytime talk show; while she and the other guests were waiting in the green room to go on, they were instructed by the producer to interrupt each other if they disagreed, and to speak forcefully rather than thoughtfully. My friend was struck by how much the show promoted conflict, contention, and negative spiritual principles, and how it cast aside civility and positive Spiritual Principles. The program deliberately encouraged noise over dialogue.

Today, the more important an issue is, the less dialogue and the more noise there seems to be. Monologue seems to be drowning out dialogue and listening; extreme positions seem to be squeezing out wholesome and sensible positions in the middle; and listening, civility, and compromise are seen as naïve. Yet when we fill up our lives up with such noise and clutter, we drown out conscience, knowingly or unknowingly. Then we can lose touch with our spiritual centers, drift off course, and fall into spiritual decay.

Free Will

The greatest spiritual gift we have is free will. As free individuals, we can choose to move beyond our instinctual responses.

If someone cuts us off in traffic, we may instinctively react with fear and anger at first. But because we have free will, we can choose to just drive on instead of clenching our fist and yelling angry words at the other driver.

Free will enables us to choose between positive Spiritual Principles and negative ones. It gives us freedom and choice, but also responsibility—all core spiritual elements. As Viktor Frankl noted, "Man exists authentically only when he is not driven but, rather, responsible." Our actions are not fate unveiling itself; they are the result of us making choices. It's because of free will that we can do good or evil deeds.

Ayn Rand observed, "Man is a being with free will; therefore, each man is potentially good or evil, and it's up to him and only him to decide which he wants to be." To be free, to choose good, we must also be able to choose evil. In practice, most of us do both. The person who cheats on her taxes may also spend a day a week volunteering at a local homeless shelter.

No one is—or ever will be—entirely good or bad. Only the morally arrogant see themselves as above doing bad deeds—and arrogance is one of the darkest negative spiritual principles.

Our good and bad choices are almost always practical, not abstract. Your spouse goes shopping for a chair and spends more than twice the amount you had agreed upon. Your instinct urges you to yell and shame him, or to manipulate the situation to get him to let you buy the new computer you want. But instead, you talk with him about your fear of falling into debt. Acting out of compassion and patience, you offer to help him return the chair and shop for a different chair within the agreed-upon price range.

Through free will, we commit to our values or betray them. We choose who we are, what we stand for, and what we become.

Our instinctual side fears the bridle of conscience and hates the responsibility that comes with free will. This is why, when we act badly, we don't want to be held responsible for our choices and actions. We use the negative spiritual principle of arrogance, or we see ourselves as a victim when clearly we are not. It is also why when we *want* to act badly, acting morally can feel like a tight collar and leash.

Because we have free will and the ability to choose both good and bad, practicing positive Spiritual Principles involves paying attention. Responsibility requires awareness. Awareness means paying attention to ourselves. It involves examining and questioning our motivations. Awareness thus makes the borders between our conscious and unconscious more fluid, allowing us to better understand our motives.

Awareness is not just an occasional practice. It's always valuable—and almost always necessary. Just because we choose to be moral today does not mean that we won't want to choose otherwise tomorrow. Thus we need ongoing awareness, vigilance, and accountability. We must be willing to continually inventory our motivations, desires, and inclinations. We may often need to stop to reflect on what we're thinking, feeling, and doing—or about to do. We may take a formal personal inventory of our conduct once a day or once a week, or go on retreats to reflect on our conduct over time. (Our instinctual side resists this self-examination, of course; it prefers to examine and judge others instead.)

To be good, we must choose to *do* good, over and over, in situation after situation. It's not a single definitive choice, but one that we make time and time again, within the messiness and difficulties of life. Action must always follow these spiritual choices; a decision without an action behind it is just a hope.

Awareness, responsibility, and free will: these form the trilogy of personal spiritual development.

Life sets events and options before us. When we run up against the unfairness of life, we will all be tempted to temporarily forget or ignore positive Spiritual Principles. Yet we must remember that we are not victims of life; we are co-creators of it.

A courageous woman whom I had the privilege of counseling was repeatedly raped by her brother as she grew up. She joined a rape support group so as not to become a victim. "Yes, he had the power to abuse me, but he doesn't have the power to make me a victim," she said. She read everything she could find about Nelson Mandela, Viktor Frankl, and others who had faced evil and chosen to wrap themselves in positive Spiritual Principles and their ethical healing powers, instead of in the illusory power of never-ending anger and hate. She chose morality over powerlessness.

We can fully and mindfully exercise our free will only when we have learned to clearly see our instinctual reactions and not get swept away by them. We can learn to slow down time by using positive Spiritual Principles such as patience, tolerance, awareness, and discipline. We then can make choices about what other positive Spiritual Principles to bring to the situation. Thus we can respond morally instead of merely reacting.

Principles before Personalities

Because positive Spiritual Principles are purer spiritual entities than we are, *positive Spiritual Principles must lead us.* These Principles must come before our personalities. If they do not, spiritual chaos follows. Unless our instinct is guided, fear and desires will become the motivations behind our actions. The animal inside us must be domesticated.

During our lives, we all have to face days of deep and seemingly endless pain, which may come in the form of fear, dread, grief, loneliness, or despair. At times, all of us are forced to go to places we would never willingly go. It is at these times that we most need positive Spiritual Principles and the people who routinely live by them. These people are the angels who can offer guidance and lead us, step by step, out of the abyss. It is especially at these times that positive Spiritual Principles need to come before personalities.

Positive Spiritual Principles are wormholes into new and wondrous worlds. The more we study them and seek to know and understand them, the more they will define and transform us.

Our instinctual side will naturally resist, but we can calmly acknowledge this resistance and continue to follow the guidance of positive Spiritual Principles.

Over time, we will come to see that meaning and importance come not from leading, but from following these Principles. We are to be the host, the student. This is the essence of practical spirituality.

SPIRITUAL PRINCIPLES
AND THE
HUMAN HEART

Our Drives for Pleasure, Power, and Meaning

When we understand that man is the only animal who must create meaning, who must open a wedge into neutral nature, we already understand the essence of love. Love is the problem of an animal who must find life, create a dialogue with nature in order to experience his own being.
—*Ernest Becker*

ONE OF THE FUNDAMENTAL DILEMMAS we face as humans is that we're half animal and half spirit. Because of our dual nature, we are imperfect beings; we are incomplete animals and incomplete spiritual beings.

Instinct vs. Spirit

My cat was a better animal than I am because he didn't feel the tension of conscience. He was pure instinct. If a mouse ran into the room, there was no moral issue for him—just a chase and a meal.

Our animal instincts—for safety, food, sex, and sleep—

serve a very basic and beneficial purpose: They keep us alive, both individually and as a species. Because they are about self-preservation, these instincts create a natural narcissism that is part of all of us.

But we humans are much more than just our instincts. We also have our spiritual side, which needs to monitor, temper, and regularly override our animal instincts.

When we fail to recognize and monitor the instinctual side of our being, and when we give it free rein, we become dangerous to both others and ourselves. When this happens, we justify excess, selfishness, entitlement, and overconsumption.

Instinct operates largely from fear. It unconsciously drives us to wonder, *Where is there danger? Where is there safety?* We humans respond to this fear in many different ways. We work to deny it. We try to distance ourselves from it. We build empires, large and small, believing that safety and control can be found in them. We seek refuge from fear in trance states. We repress fear. We cling to naïve beliefs, hoping that our innocence will protect us. We attack others or work to defeat them. We try to transfer our fears onto others with blame and anger.

Our instincts are part of us, but they do not fully define us. As Teilhard de Chardin observed, "We are not human beings having a spiritual experience, but spiritual beings having a human experience." Our spiritual side is part of the Divine—that collective, universal sense of decency and morality that lives deep inside all of us, and that will guide us toward love, care, and healing. This side of us realizes that we are much more than a separate self. Often, it asks that we sacrifice a piece of that self for the good of something much larger. When we act only from instinct, we ignore Spirit and the demands that positive Spiritual Principles make of us.

The easiest way for us to transcend the limits of our instincts—our ego—is to live according to positive Spiritual Principles and put them into practice in our everyday lives.

Positive Spiritual Principles are timeless. Respect, dignity, justice, equality, and others were worthy goals hundreds of years ago, and they will remain just as worthy hundreds of years from now.

Through these positive Spiritual Principles, we transcend and transform our instincts. Used as guides, these principles enable us to find and connect with humanity and the Divine. They also help us to be—and feel—less alone.

It isn't bad that we have instincts and animal desires. They're natural parts of us. What matters is what we do with them and the choices we make regarding them. Indeed, the fact that we can stand up to them, work with them, and detach from them is what makes us spiritual beings. By integrating yet rising above our instinctual desires, we discover meaning, create meaningful relationships, and live meaningful lives.

The natural tension between our instinctual and spiritual sides is quite valuable to us. It forces us to use our free will to make choices and to be responsible for those choices and their consequences.

When we move beyond our instinctual resistance and incorporate positive Spiritual Principles into our lives, we find ourselves able to do things we would have never believed we could do. As a client I worked with told me, "Through living by the vows my wife and I took when we got married, I became a better man than I could have ever dreamed of." Another client, now a loving grandmother, said, "When I found out I was pregnant at age sixteen, I knew nothing of how to be a mother. I cried and panicked for three days. Then I told myself I would do everything I could to avoid becoming another neglectful or abusive mother, like the other women in my family. I found a mother mentor who taught me how to be a good, loving mother. I vowed to stop the abuse and not pass it on. I knew I had been successful when my daughter graduated from college and found a respectful, wonderful man for her husband.

When she became pregnant, I cried tears of joy, not tears of fear and panic."

Choosing to Attach and Detach

As humans, we have the ability to attach to—or form relationships with—ideas, concepts, self, and others. But, just as we have the ability to *attach*, we also have the ability to *detach* from ideas, concepts, self, and others. This detachment is a uniquely human capability. Animals can't detach from instinct, but, being half Spirit, we can.

Thus we have choices in every moment of our lives. We get to decide what path we will take, what positive Spiritual Principles or negative spiritual principles we will follow, what kind of person we will be, and what we will make of our lives.

However, this ability to detach is a double-edged sword. *We also have the ability to attach to or detach from our spiritual side.* Part of our work as human beings is to stay attached to positive Spiritual Principles, even when our instincts tempt us not to.

The dance of being human is often a dance of attachment and detachment. If our spouse says something that sparks fear in us, our fear may tell us to fight back, run, or play naïve. At the same time, however, our spiritual side asks us to let go of our reaction, to look past our fear, to listen to what our spouse is saying, and to connect with him mindfully and lovingly.

Detaching from our instincts causes our energy and perspective to shift. We disrupt the flow of energy to our ego and instinct, and can then consciously attach it to positive Spiritual Principles. This, in turn, helps us stay focused, work through our fears, and attain our goals.

Over time, we become whatever we most often attach to, and we don't become what we detach from. If we work hard to stay attached to the Principle of integrity, for example, over time we become a person of integrity. If we work to stay attached to the negative principle of cynicism, over time we become a cynic. If we learn to place positive Spiritual Principles before instinctual desire, we grow and mature.

We can consciously work to live more spiritual, moral lives. In order to do this, however, we need to understand three basic human drives.

Three Basic Drives: Pleasure, Power, and Meaning

A *drive* is an emotional, physical, and/or spiritual desire strong enough to lead us to act in certain ways. In humans, these three basic drives are the drive for pleasure, the drive for power, and the drive for meaning. We need all three drives if we are to develop as spiritual beings.

Our first two drives—the drive for power and the drive for pleasure—are instinctual. We share these drives with other animals. The third drive—the drive for meaning—derives from our spiritual side. We all have these three drives, and our energy regularly moves from one to another as we go about our lives. How we weave these three drives together determines who we become and what type of life we put together.

Each drive gives us a different view of the world, a different sense of what holds importance, and a different energy. Let's look at how each drive affects our relationships with other people.

Through our drive for pleasure, we see that relationships can be sources of pleasurable feelings and fun. This drive draws us to people who make us feel good and urges us to avoid people around whom we feel bad.

Through our drive for power, we see relationships as hierarchical. This drive encourages us to seek people who support our positions and views, who can help us climb up the social or professional ladder, or who offer us an opportunity to achieve or get something—money or status, for example. This drive also pushes us to control others.

Through our drive for meaning, we see relationships as essential to creating meaning in our lives and to accessing higher, healing truths. Our drive for meaning shows us that we all are incomplete, and that through meaningful and challenging relationships, we'll develop a deeper and more accurate view of life. Our drive for meaning opens us to be curious about who can help us, guide us, and teach us. It sees each person as having a unique and meaningful story that we can learn from.

These three drives usually don't get along very well. For starters, there is the issue of which drive will lead us. Typically, the drives push against each other, jockeying for position. Each one wants to dominate. Our instinctual drives for power and pleasure have an advantage because they come naturally and easily to us. Both of these drives are willing to avoid, sacrifice, or betray positive Spiritual Principles in order to get what they desire.

Here are a couple of common examples:

1. *On her way home from work, Emily stops at the local casino, throwing into the slot machines a few dollars that she can't afford to lose. In the process, she sacrifices some dignity and energy that would be better used to relate with her family. But that hour of gambling feels good and helps her forget the pressures of her day.*

2. *Jerome works many extra hours in order to get promoted in his company. In the process, he sacrifices meaningful connections with his family and friends. Though his wife complains about his long hours and says she'd rather have him around more, he tells himself that she'll sing a*

*different tune when he gets his promotion and the money
that comes with it.*

Our drives for pleasure and power naturally attract us to
negative spiritual principles such as greed, control, cynicism,
and self-righteousness. The sensations they create—as well as
the ones they spur us to chase after—can be very seductive.

It's not easy to put our drive for meaning in the lead. The
other two drives naturally lead us to resist that effort. Sorting
out what is meaningful and right frustrates our animal side,
which desires immediate satisfaction and control. It also involves sacrificing some of our wants and desires in the pursuit
of higher Spiritual Principles. Yet in order to compose a meaningful life, we need to put our drive for meaning in the lead
position, because this is the part of us that understands, con-
nects with, interacts with, and responds to positive Spiritual
Principles. Our drive for meaning also understands the need
for and the value of sacrifice and delayed gratification. This
drive can help us keep tabs on our drive for pleasure—not by
squelching it, but by promoting richness, sensuality, and fun in
ways that nurture and restore us, while causing no harm. Our
drive for meaning can also direct our drive for power to help us
do good and make a positive difference in the world.

Paradoxically, when we put our drive for meaning in
charge, our life becomes more pleasurable and more powerful
because we create *ethical* power and *ethical* pleasure. Indeed,
our drive for meaning would be powerless and joyless without
the juice that comes from our drives for pleasure and power.

Let's take a closer look at each of these three drives.

Our Drive for Pleasure

Our drive for pleasure loves positive physical sensations:
the smell of roses, the touch of a lover's embrace, the sound

of good music, the taste of good food, the feel of warm sunshine on our skin, the shade of a big tree on a summer day, the breeze on our face as we ride a bicycle, star-filled skies, rainbows, fine fabrics, a cozy evening fire.

These are good things. We need pleasure, and our drive for pleasure makes sure we get some. It always, however, makes us want *more*, and want it *now.* But *more* and *now* are a dangerous combination. If we focus on fulfilling these desires instead of moderating and guiding them, we get out of balance. We push ourselves deeper into our appetites and further away from the Divine. We chase sensations instead of doing the next right thing. We also make ourselves vulnerable to anything or anyone that promises to satisfy our appetites. And the more we try to satisfy our appetite at the expense of Spirit, the more Spirit longs to be set free.

Sometimes we misinterpret this spiritual longing as a desire for still more pleasurable sensations. We then risk falling into an orgy of consumption and self-indulgence.

Yet the pursuit of pleasure quickly becomes self-defeating. All pleasure is made up of sensations, and all sensations eventually fade away. Chasing pleasure for pleasure's sake is ultimately unsatisfying. You can experience pleasure for a moment, but its effects do not last, and you end up frustrated and disappointed.

Nevertheless, it is also through our drive for pleasure that we feel the joy, gratitude, love, and serenity that come from bringing positive Spiritual Principles to life. Our spiritual side wants pleasure for ourselves, but it also wants to add pleasure into the world. This is the essence of service to and for others. As we put our ego aside to help others in self-sacrificing ways, we let others know that someone cares, we let *ourselves* know we care, and we touch the best of what we are.

My friend Joe, who regularly volunteers for Habitat for Humanity, often speaks of the joy he gets from his efforts: "I love driving by the homes we built months or years ago, seeing children playing on the lawns, and knowing that in some small way I was part of something good." Such self-sacrifice for the good of others opens chambers in our hearts that hold deep, ancient love.

It's easy to see how our drive for pleasure can get us in trouble when pleasure becomes a goal in and of itself, or when pleasure alone defines us. A second, less obvious danger is when we make suffering or self-sacrifice into a goal.

Neither pleasure nor pain should be a goal; these come as natural by-products of the choices we make and the lives we lead. The pure pursuit of pleasure—or pain—is a choice of self over spirit, personality over principle.

Our drive for pleasure seeks to protect us from pain, and that's usually a good thing. But the drive for pleasure can also encourage us to try to avoid all pain, including necessary pain, such as grief at the loss of a friend, or the soreness that comes from a good workout, or the pain of healing from important surgery. Our drive for pleasure may also push us to avoid the minor discomfort that comes from meeting new people, learning new ideas and behaviors, and encountering unfamiliar cultures and situations. This knee-jerk avoidance can turn into spiritual indifference, inertia, or an unwillingness to change.

Practical spirituality requires that we accept necessary pain and suffering, allowing them to transform us into better people rather than better avoiders. Some suffering must not be avoided; some suffering we must directly walk into and embrace. For example, if we choose to love others, we will experience pain and sacrifice on a regular basis. And reaching a goal requires work—sometimes more than we feel like doing. A good education, for example, is achieved largely through hard work and an openness to new ideas.

Viktor Frankl described two types of suffering: *avoidable suffering*, which we can and should choose to avoid, and *unavoidable suffering*, those tragedies and adversities that are placed irrevocably on our path. I would add another type of suffering: *chosen suffering*. Chosen suffering is suffering we need to embrace in order to fully develop as human, spiritual beings. Here are some examples: (1) You spend weekends studying at the library to attain your goal of getting a 4.0 grade-point average in college, even though your friends are partying and regularly invite you to join them. (2) You have both knees replaced so you can continue to go hiking with your grandchildren. (3) You put together an intervention for your drug-addicted brother, knowing he will be furious with you.

When we accept and face unavoidable suffering, we often feel incomplete and vulnerable. This is when we most need positive Spiritual Principles. They can help guide us through the pain. They can help us clarify what our anguish is about, what we are to learn from it, and what we need in order to heal. As a result, they can transform our pain.

Our Drive for Power

Power is about potential: our potential to do and be good, or to create misery for others and ourselves.

Power and our sense of self are intimately intertwined. When we are born, our first breath puts us on a journey to develop our potential into some form of power. But will we seek power based only on negative spiritual principles and our ability to dominate and create fear in others? Or will we choose ethical power, the power of positive Spiritual Principles?

Power, like pleasure, is inherently neither good nor bad. We can access and wield power based on our values and highest aspirations, or on our desires and fears. As Eric Hoffer explained in his book *The Passionate State of Mind,* "It is when power is wedded to chronic fear that it becomes formidable"—and, I would add, dangerous and easy to misuse. When power is guided by our fears and desires, we only generate suffering, not only for ourselves, but also for others, as we work to place our fears onto and into them.

Power needs to be contained within and guided by positive Spiritual Principles if it is to be transformed into its highest form, ethical power. Ethical power is sacred power. It can heal and transform individuals, groups, institutions, nations, and cultures. Yet ethical power is fundamentally humble; it doesn't seek status or prestige.

Our drive for power is closely tied to our survival. It makes us react quickly and intensely to any fear or perceived danger. Thus we need the guidance and leadership that positive Spiritual Principles can provide. Principles such as patience, tolerance, and humility slow down natural fear reactions, allowing us to respond wisely to situations instead of instinctively reacting to them.

Our drive for power seeks to protect us from dangers, both real and imagined. When this drive senses danger, it spurs us to put up defenses and isolate ourselves from whatever that danger may be. This drive is inherently selfish. It doesn't understand the concept of self-sacrifice, but it believes in sacrificing others. When we argue with our partner, it is our drive for power that demands that they admit they are wrong. At its worst, it may demand they admit their inherent wrongness as a person.

Our drive for power likes power that can be felt and seen, power we can wrap our hands around. It understands the sensations of *raw power* more than the concept of *ethical power*. It prefers the fist to the hug, the scream to the debate, the sword to peaceful compromise. It also likes noise, for noise makes it hard to hear the subtle voice and demands of conscience.

Without the guidance of positive Spiritual Principles, our drive for power can coax us into a "me vs. others" mentality, and into disconnection from anything that doesn't satisfy our desire for more.

Influenced by our drive for power, we often see isolation as a solution. Think of a time when you were in a heated argument with someone close to you. Was there a soft—or loud— voice inside you that said, *I don't need this crap, I don't need this person, either. I'd be so much better off alone?* I joke with my wife that there are days when I want to trade her for a puppy, knowing that the next day I would mortgage everything to get her back. This is my drive for power offering up its standard, predictable response.

Our drive for power leads us to resist change because change is unpredictable. It causes us to see change as risky and thus fear it. In order to change, we must offer up some part of us; we must be willing to become different. Our beliefs and perspectives must be transformed. This doesn't make sense to our drive for power. It tells us that there is nothing wrong with us, that our beliefs and actions are proper and correct, and that there's no need for us to change. The world and others need to change, not us. They are what's wrong; we are what's right.

Spirituality asks us to always be ready and willing to sacrifice, to surrender our instinctual ego to higher principles and purposes. But blinded by our drive for power, we see no purpose higher than self-preservation, which means protecting our beliefs, our way of seeing and being in the world, our own personal status quo.

Our drive for power is thus primarily antirelationship. It is suspicious of all authentic, loving relationships because other people may challenge us or be unwilling to let us be in control.

The relationships our drive for power does find comforting are those in which the other person's beliefs, fears, and wants are exactly the same as ours. It leads us to think: *If you are the same as me, you are not a threat to me. We can be alone together, connected through our shared mistrust, anger, and fears.* Ideas or people that our drive for power doesn't understand are thus seen as villains to be mistrusted, defended against, and, perhaps, attacked or destroyed. This drive then justifies its own self-centeredness by declaring and focusing on the perceived wrongness of others.

Our instinctual drive for power seduces us into finding some pleasure in the suffering of others. Bullies love to see their own fear transferred onto someone else's face. The abusive parent finds satisfaction when his child runs to his room crying, for now the anger and pain that live inside the parent live within the child as well. Terrorists take pleasure in watching news coverage of the massive suffering they have created. They feel satisfied when the hate they feel inside becomes a hatred directed back at them.

Our drive for power would have us believe in the fantasy that security lies in control. Left untethered, our drive for power can turn both others and ourselves into soulless objects to be manipulated, without regard for the consequences.

To our drive for power, right and wrong have little to do with truth, and everything to do with dominance and submission. Might makes right. If I have power over you, then I'm right and you are wrong—and now you have to carry the fear, not me.

To our drive for power, the people who have the most power naturally have the right to lead, the right to carry the banner of truth, and the right to dominate and (if necessary) humiliate others.

Alternatively, we may feel that we alone stand proudly and defiantly against the status quo, the powers that be, or the world. Yet our pride, defiance, and bravado are in fact thin veneers over dependent relationships with the negative spiritual principles of cynicism, intolerance, and unmanaged fear.

Fortunately, we can monitor ourselves and recognize when

we are operating (or tempted to operate) from our drive for power. Here are some warning signs: We have a strong desire to be in control or to be right. We want others to acknowledge that we are right. We generally mistrust others. We feel self-righteous. We want others to suffer. We feel like a victim and that others don't understand us. We're afraid most or all of the time. We find ourselves angry at most everything and everyone. We react to or feel annoyed by little things. We are full of resentment, seeing only our side of things.

By applying positive Spiritual Principles, we can discipline and domesticate our drive for power. Guided by them, we seek to *heal* wounds, not deepen them or pass them on to others. These Principles call us to *surrender,* not *submit,* to the care and love that Spirit holds. Through this surrender, we can turn our drive for power into a force of goodness. We can move beyond willfulness into willingness.

Our Drive for Meaning

Spirituality is about forming a loving partnership among of all three of our basic drives, with our drive for meaning in the lead.

We need the passion embedded in our drive for pleasure, and we need the perseverance and dedication that can be found in our drive for power. But both of these aspects of our humanness need to be led and mentored by our drive for meaning. When we place meaning before power and pleasure, we are able to transcend our instinctual selves, keep our ego in check, and put principles before personality.

We also experience a change in perspective. Negative spiritual principles create rigid perspectives; positive Spiritual Principles allow fluidity, creativity, openness, and curiosity.

As Rollo May observed, "Life comes from physical survival; but the good life comes from what we care about." Our drive for meaning is what makes us care about things that hold Spirit. It helps us to enjoy the uncertainty of the question mark instead of seeing it as a threat. It seeks transformation instead of the status quo.

Our drive for meaning doesn't come from our instincts, but from our fears, our doubts, our agony, our suffering, and our incompleteness. Our drive for meaning creates in us a willingness to embrace our incompleteness, a desire to be transformed, and a longing to connect with something larger and more meaningful than ourselves. Through it, we respond to our own darkness with a desire to seek the light, and we respond to our character defects with a yearning to develop character.

Unlike all other animals, we humans don't just want relief from our current suffering; we want to *understand* our suffering and learn from it. Our journey into meaning starts when we begin to realize that we are in control of little, that we have few answers, that we often don't even know the right questions, and that we have—and always will have—much more to learn.

Our drive for meaning often turns us into spiritual pilgrims who search for the sacred. It keeps us seeking, discovering, and rediscovering ever deeper, more illuminating, and more healing truths. At the same time, it reminds us that our own understanding of truth will always be incomplete, and that anyone who claims they can give us the complete, absolute truth is focused on power instead of meaning.

Each of us must discover our own meaning and our own place in the world; others can't dictate these to us. Indeed, the drive for meaning takes no one standard form; it has a slightly different shape for each of us. Others can help us, but we must make our own discoveries, then share our stories of discovery with others.

Similarly, we cannot discover meaning for anyone else. We can offer our experience and guidance, but meaning can never be handed from one person to another. It can't—and shouldn't—be forced or inflicted on others, either.

Our drive for meaning is multidimensional, not one-dimensional. Unlike our drives for power and pleasure, it can help us step back, reflect, and ask, *What am I to learn from this? Why is this happening to me? How can I be better because of this? How can I help make my community a better place because of this?* It also often guides us to ask, *What is the wisest and most caring way to act in this situation?* The quality of our spirituality comes from how we answer these and other, similar questions.

We do not start out seeking meaning as children. We start out wanting pleasure and safety. The pursuit of meaning comes later, as our parents, teachers, relatives, mentors, and friends lead us—and at times push us—toward it. We watch and interact with our families, and from these first interactions we learn a hierarchy of pleasure, power, and meaning—which comes first, which second, and which last. Some families are meaning-based, but many are power-based, and some are pleasure-based. Because of free will, however, each of us gets to create our own hierarchy of pleasure, power, and meaning when we reach adulthood.

In order to discover meaning, we must be willing to sacrifice homeostasis—our usual balance and our personal status quo. Our drive for meaning thus makes us willing to give up comfort and familiarity for the possibility of more meaning. We become interested in other people and their stories, other cultures, other religions, other ideas, other ways of being, and other ways of seeing the world.

The main hallmark of our drive for meaning is its capacity for inclusiveness. It brings to light the strength and beauty of diversity, the potential that lies within our differences, and the learning and sharing that these differences can provide. As my good friend Kathi says, "It's not the notes that make music beautiful; it's the spaces between them."

Our drive for meaning shows us that everything and everyone has something to teach us. Meaning is thus deeply inclusive, excluding only those forces that seek to do harm. Meaning always has room for those who seek it and are willing to work for it. All who need healing are welcome to feel its embrace.

Through meaning, we create intimacy and a reciprocal relationship with positive Spiritual Principles. As we validate these Principles through our actions, we in turn are validated: care begets care, respect begets respect, honesty begets honesty, love begets love.

The Interplay of Meaning and Power

When something happens, meaning drives us to ask, *What is this about? What is the meaning within this?* It makes us curious; it makes us want to learn. It keeps us open to the world and to the Divine.

In contrast, power declares, *The meaning of this is . . .* Power makes pronouncements and judges things as true or not true; it finds comfort in finality and self-assuredness.

Our drive for power makes us believe in and seek control, while our drive for meaning allows us to accept that we can never have control, only limited influence, and sometimes no influence at all. Through power, we interpret fear as a loss of control, a crisis that demands that we seek and gain more control. Through meaning, however, we see fears as fragile veils to be pushed aside in order to strengthen our relationships with positive Spiritual Principles.

With our drive for power at the helm, we resist personal change, for we see ourselves as unflawed and complete. Through our drive for power, we believe that it's the world and others who are wrong. But through our drive for meaning, we see ourselves as incomplete, continually evolving, and needing ongoing monitoring and managing. Our spiritual side has no shame about being incomplete. It understands that incompleteness is an element of being human. But through our drive for power, we experience shame and embarrassment when our incompleteness is exposed.

Combining Our Drives into Spiritual Harmony

Living with all three of these drives can be maddening at times, especially if we have not resolved the issue of which drive will lead us. An internal debate develops, and we may feel conflicted, confused, anxious, regretful, or disconnected from the life we are trying to put together. This internal debate needs to be resolved in order for us not to feel separate from ourselves.

The vast majority of the time, our drive for meaning needs to lead and guide our other two basic drives. But the other drives do get—and need—to express themselves. For example, when we're on vacation, we need to have fun and indulge our drive for pleasure, but we still need to stay within our value system. When you're playing football with your nephews, it's okay to let out that competitive drive for power so you can beat their behinds, but even during these times you need your drive for meaning to guide, direct, and temper your emotions. This keeps you from tackling them so hard that you injure them, or calling them nasty names when they score.

Spiritual harmony is not the mere coexistence of instinct and Spirit. Spiritual harmony is created when instinct and Spirit combine to operate as one interdependent unit, like the voices of a choir or a smoothly functioning sports team. We see beyond our personal desires; ethical power gets released; and we know and experience ourselves as enough. In the process, feelings of loneliness disappear.

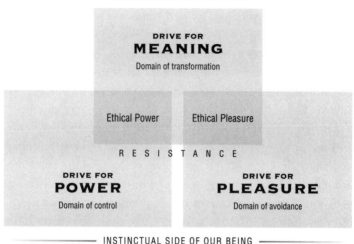

SPIRITUAL SIDE OF OUR BEING

DRIVE FOR
MEANING
Domain of transformation

Ethical Power   Ethical Pleasure

R E S I S T A N C E

DRIVE FOR   **DRIVE FOR**
POWER   ## PLEASURE
Domain of control   Domain of avoidance

INSTINCTUAL SIDE OF OUR BEING

Although our three basic drives often struggle against each other, our drive for meaning recognizes that meaning is often found within that very struggle, as well as within life's other challenges. Thus our drive for meaning encourages us to step into, rather than avoid, these struggles and challenges.

The tension among our three drives, "the committee inside our heads," is not only normal, but also helpful, because it creates essential energy. We can discipline this energy and channel it through our drive for meaning—our spiritual side—where we combine it with positive Spiritual Principles in order to do the next right thing. In doing so, we can create ethical power and ethical pleasure, the highest forms of power and pleasure we humans can create on our own.

Power Struggles vs. Integrity

As we human beings interact, we will always have issues and problems to work through. When these appear, we may instinctively feel afraid. How we deal with this fear is of great importance. If we send it over to instinct, we will react from our drive for pleasure and try to distance ourselves from whatever we see as the cause of the fear. We may also react from our drive for power and become either defensive or aggressive.

If both people in a conflict react from instinct, then this collision of instincts creates a power struggle in which each side seeks to dominate the other. One person may submit to the other; resentments may get created; one person may win and the other may lose; both may walk away in an emotional stalemate. In each such case, however, no genuine solutions are created. Solutions are never the outcome of power struggles. There may be decisions and temporary accommodations, but no solutions. In power struggles, each side abandons Spirit for instinct, hoping to win a point.

If instead, however, each person applies positive Spiritual Principles to the conflict, an entirely different dynamic emerges. Each person acknowledges that they and their way of viewing the issue are part of the problem. Each is willing to alter or sacrifice part of their view to resolve the conflict. Each also monitors themselves and their conduct throughout this process. Both sides put aside self-importance and the desire for victory and control in favor of creating a workable solution that both find satisfactory. Instead of struggling against each other, both people struggle to resolve the conflict together. This enables them to stay connected throughout the conflict, and to bring out the best of each other.

SPIRITUAL PRINCIPLES AND THE BRAIN

The triune (Greek, meaning "three-in-one") brain theory was developed by Paul MacLean, M.D. (1913–2007). MacLean was chief neuroscientist at the Laboratory of Brain Evolution and Behavior at the National Institute of Mental Health from 1971 to 1985. While elements of this theory—especially the "reptilian brain" concept—have been challenged by more recent research, I present it here as a model I've found useful in exploring the interplay of positive Spiritual Principles and negative spiritual principles.

According to this theory, our brains are made up of three unique structures. Each serves a different function, each sees and interacts with the world in a unique way, and each structure has its own special kind of intelligence. How we interact with and view others depends on which structure dominates at any given moment.

These three parts of MacLean's model of the brain are called the *reptilian brain* or the *R-complex,* the *limbic system,* and the *neocortex.* Think of them as operating like three interconnected biological computers. These three structures correspond closely to our three drives for power, pleasure, and meaning, respectively. The descriptions that follow are not meant so much to reflect current brain science, but more as my creative interpretations of MacLean's triune model to give you a way to think about your brain's role in processing positive and negative principles.

THE REPTILIAN BRAIN

We can see this as a metaphor for the part of the brain concerned with survival and safety—the brain of fight, flee, or freeze. This is the part of us that makes us jump, in what is called the startle response, when we hear a loud noise or sense some danger.

Think of this part of our brain as very territorial and preverbal, so it mainly monitors and responds to tones and body language. It is concerned primarily with issues of safety.

The reptilian brain can take over the rest of the brain when it senses danger, whether real or perceived—and it often interprets fear, sadness, or a sense of powerlessness as danger. The reptilian brain is easily frustrated. It also holds the potential for violence. This part of the brain does not look into the future. It is designed to deal only with what is right in front of us. *It also does not learn from past mistakes.* A reptilian brain is not relational, only instinctual. It sees relationships only in terms of mating. And because morality only takes place in the context of relationships, this part of our brain is basically amoral. It rebels against surrendering to moral standards. Instead, it operates in terms of power, domination, and submission.

The reptilian brain views conscience as a burden. Conscience speaks of values and relationships, and this part of our brain wants little to do with either. But it is attracted to power, status, and prestige, and it likes to chase after them.

When we suffer trauma, our reptilian brain kicks in. We may then look for people and institutions that we feel are powerful and in control, in the hope that they will protect us. We may also seek chemicals or behaviors that help *us* feel in control and powerful. We may hoard things or cling to beliefs in order to feel safe and secure.

People who operate primarily from their reptilian brains often use their power to push others into their own reptilian brains— their anger, their fears, and their reactivity—making those people easier to manipulate or dismiss.

THE LIMBIC SYSTEM

In this model, the limbic system is called the *paleomammalian brain*—and, sometimes, the *mammal brain.* It is our pleasure center, as well as the seat of our senses, our emotions, and our desires for relationships with others. If someone yells "Fire!" the reptilian part of our brain may get us out of the building, but our limbic system may play a part in making us run back in for the child, pet, or photo album still inside.

Our emotional memories are stored in our limbic system; the stronger the emotions attached to a memory, the more clearly we remember it. For example, most of us in the United States can remember with great detail and emotion where we were on the morning of September 11, 2001. How many other Tuesday mornings in September of that year do you remember?

Picture your limbic system as sitting between your reptilian brain and your neocortex, monitoring information coming from both the external world (via our senses) and our internal world. It continually compares the information from these two sources of information to see if they match up. If the information is sensed as congruent, it is taken in, sent up, and processed through the neocortex. If the information does not match up, however, your reptilian brain is put in charge to protect us from perceived dangers.

Like the reptilian brain, we can think of this part of us as being more attracted to sensations than to abstract ideas, such as principles. However, our limbic system can work with our neocortex, where abstract thought is processed much more easily than in our reptilian brain. This allows our passions and our values to be combined into a powerful force, thanks to the third part of the triune brain, the neocortex.

THE NEOCORTEX

Our thinking brain, the neocortex, makes up about five-sixths of our brain. It surrounds our limbic and reptilian brains—and, with proper training, it has the power to overrule them.

The neocortex deals with concepts, symbols, and language. It looks for patterns and likes relationships. It also likes to plan and to solve problems; it's the logical part of our brain. Our neocortex seeks to answer the question *Why?* It's the part of the brain that seeks meaning.

There's a special part of the neocortex that looks into the future and imagines alternatives. This part of our neocortex, the *prefrontal lobe*, asks, *What if?* It also creates options, knowing that in the long run, the more options a person, group, or community has, the better.

The prefrontal lobe works to guide, and at times control, the impulsive, instinctual parts of our brain. It often struggles with our reptilian brain because values, morals, and impulse controls only cramp the reptilian brain's style.

Our reptilian brain and limbic system are deeply attracted to sensations. But because our neocortex is even more attracted to finding meaning, it plays the key role in our ability to live according to positive Spiritual Principles, and to translate those principles into action. But our neocortex also needs the energies and passions found within the limbic system and reptilian brain in order to create a practical spirituality and a dedication to values.

How does our story end? These three brains, living within one mind, need to develop into a harmonious team, with positive Spiritual Principles coaching and guiding them through the trials and fears that life often generates.

Personal Value Systems

Each of us has our own value system—our personal collection of relationships with negative spiritual principles and positive Spiritual Principles. This value system is a living, fluid entity that guides our decisions and actions.

A value conflict occurs when our instinctual side and our spiritual side, represented by different parts of our brain, look at a situation and have differing views on what is important about it and what to do about it.

It is natural to regularly have these conflicts. What is most important is how we resolve them and which side we fall on—instinct or Spirit.

Most of us have two value systems: a spoken value system, the one we tell to others and ourselves ("I believe in this," "These are principles I live by"), and a behavioral value system, the one we actually live by—the one reflected in our decisions and actions. Our behavioral value system is the truest mirror we can look into, and it's what I mean when I use the term *personal value system*. Our behavioral value system reveals both the negative spiritual principles and the positive Spiritual Principles we live by.

Any personal value system naturally works to preserve itself and keep its systems in balance—in a state of homeostasis. This tendency toward balance is amoral; once a balance is established, it produces tension or anxiety when something upsets that balance. This tension can be intense, but more often it is subtle.

This tension encourages us to return to our normal balance. In this way, all change is resisted by the system, and our personal value system can hinder any change we want or need to make.

For example, let's imagine that you spend all your free time on the Internet and very little with your family. You want to change, so you tell yourself, *No Internet once I get home from work*. You do well for the first week. Then you think, *Well, I can go on the Net once the kids go to sleep*. A week after that, you tell yourself, *The children are busy watching their favorite show*, so you go on the computer just for a little bit. Slowly, over a period of two months, you revert to your old habits—your value system's old normal. The status quo of the system has won out.

This is why discipline is one of the most important positive Spiritual Principles: we may need to exercise it for months, or even years, to change an ingrained system of thought and action and to become the person we want to be.

PART II

LIVING the PRINCIPLES

SPIRITUAL GROWTH
ON A
CONTINUUM

41 Pairs of Spiritual Principles

EACH POSITIVE SPIRITUAL PRINCIPLE has its negative counterpart. Each pair is part of a continuum, with the negative spiritual principles at one end. Interestingly, however, each continuum has no positive endpoint, because positive Spiritual Principles are boundless, continuing on forever.

We find and create our moral compass as we move further in the direction of positive Spiritual Principles and lessen our dependence on (and corruption by) negative spiritual principles. Free will in the form of choices, exercised through action, moves us along these continua. Taken together, these continua create a map of our moral and spiritual journey.

The more we organize our lives around negative spiritual principles, the more fear and confusion they create, the more they will come to possess us, and the more likely we are to be tied to the material world and focused on possessing others and things. When we practice and repeat negative spiritual principles, they eventually harden and become character defects.

The beauty of all character defects, however, is that at the bottom of each is a door. If opened, this door will lead us back into the world of positive Spiritual Principles and transform us, because often we become aware of our true spiritual value only through these defects of character.

The more we organize our lives around positive Spiritual Principles, the more we are released from self-centeredness and compulsion. Because positive Spiritual Principles contain and express the Divine, they seek to release us from servitude to the material world.

Positive Spiritual Principles help us see beyond ourselves, touch the eternal, know we are not alone, and find comfort in our own imperfections. Yet positive Spiritual Principles offer us more challenge than rest, more questions than answers, more participation than isolation, more joy than excitement, more self-evaluation than self-aggrandizement. None of these positive Spiritual Principles can be controlled; they can only be embraced or ignored. The choice is ours.

Although I've presented these principles as forty-one separate pairs, they're actually aspects of a single Divine force. Our task is to see this and understand that we are both the good of the world and the evil of the world. If you wish to see an angel, look within your own heart; if you wish to see a devil, also look within your heart. We naturally split things in two, forgetting that they come from the same source. Spirituality is about seeing and claiming the connections.

Nevertheless, it remains true that positive Spiritual Principles create spiritual awakenings; negative spiritual principles create spiritual narcolepsy. Over time, the results of these choices become our personalities.

Let's examine each of these sets of spiritual principles— both the positive and the negative ones—more closely.

Judgmentalism	Openness

Judgmentalism

It's so easy to be judgmental. As we drive down the road, we find ourselves judging the driving of others. *You're too slow. You're too fast. Stop talking on the phone, you jerk. Jeez, lady, stop eating that sandwich while you drive.* At the supermarket, we look in the cart of the person in front of us. *Boy, look at all that junk food. No wonder she's so heavy.* We can get judgmental just sitting on a park bench. *Look at that guy glued to his iPad and ignoring this gorgeous sunset right in front of his eyes. Man, doesn't that kid's mom know he needs to wear a helmet? You know, the benches in Highland Park are way better than these cracked old things.*

Our reptilian brain finds comfort and safety in judgments—especially in the finality and false self-assuredness that accompany them. We exchange a question mark for a period and can become seduced into a false sense of completion.

Judgments shut us down, close our minds, neutralize our openness, and tend to push us toward absolutes. When judging, we accept only our own way of being and see other ways as inferior or just plain wrong.

Judgments close us off from others, creating separateness instead of connection. In rushing to judgment, we move toward instincts instead of toward Spirit.

Our reptilian brain always sees things as either safe or dangerous and has to make judgments quickly. Survival demands this. This is why judgmentalism is so sharp, sudden, and reactive. If we step back and observe our own minds carefully, however, we can feel this shift when it occurs. We can then interrupt the process and redirect our response through our neocortex.

We often fall into judgments when we're afraid—or when we want to create a sense of power or control. A friend recently told me, "When my wife says something that scares or challenges me, my first and most natural reaction is to judge what she said as wrong, and then search for ways to *prove* her wrongness. My second, less natural reaction is to realize that I'm afraid—and that I don't have to blame her or transfer my fear onto her."

Underneath our judgmentalism we'll usually find fear or sadness or a sense of powerlessness or some combination of these. Most violence arises from judgment and is rationalized through it.

Openness

We create openness when we put aside our judgments, manage our fears and our impulsive nature, and accept challenges and difficulties.

When we stay open, we make room for others—and their stories, their experiences, their knowledge, and their relationships with the world. Openness also allows our energies to stay fluid and gives us easier and greater access to other positive Spiritual Principles.

Openness is learned behavior. We begin practicing it when we let our curiosity trump our fear. Instead of looking at something new or unfamiliar as a threat—which is how our reptilian brain sees it—we consciously investigate that new, unfamiliar thing. (If it *does* turn out to be genuinely dangerous, we'll realize this very quickly.)

When our partner is upset with us, our reptilian brain tells us to defend ourselves—or, perhaps, to launch a verbal attack. Instead of following this message, however, we can be curious about why our partner is upset and what she is feeling. We can then ask her to tell us more. This creates connection instead of conflict. What our partner tells us may also help us to better understand her—and ourselves.

Openness is thus a spiritual achievement. It involves stepping past emotions such as sadness and fear, and past defenses such as anger, blame, and suspicion.

Being open doesn't mean believing or accepting everything that everyone says. Instead, it means being curious about why they are saying it. As an addiction counselor, I don't believe some of the things my clients tell me, but I listen openly to learn about them, to discover how they feel, and to find out what's going on for them behind their words.

To learn we need an open mind. To learn spiritual lessons, we need an open mind and an open heart.

Dave's Story

My client Dave was a World War II vet who drank to get away from the memories of what he had seen and the people he had killed. He once told me, "The worst part of having to kill another person is knowing that you're killing a little part of yourself."

As a good soldier, Dave had been trained to think of every German as an enemy. He was taught that Germans were evil and corrupt, and that they deserved to be killed by Allied soldiers. As one of the tragic necessities of war, judgmentalism was drummed into him.

Dave was especially haunted by the memory of one German

soldier he shot and killed. As Dave rolled the body over, the man's wallet fell open. There Dave saw a picture of the man, his wife, and his two children. Dave had an identical picture—of himself, his wife, and his two children, positioned in the same way— in his own wallet.

In that moment, Dave's judgmentalism and separateness fell away. He and the man he had killed were identical: two regular guys doing what they had to do. At that moment, the dead soldier stopped being the evil enemy and became just another man trying to stay alive and get back to his family.

Dave took the photo out of the dead soldier's wallet and put it in his own pocket. Later, he would often take it out and look at it when drinking.

Dave knew that war sometimes forces us to do difficult, even terrible things. In war, each side works to destroy the soul of the other, even as its own soul is attacked. He did not regret following orders or killing German soldiers. In fact, he later shot several others. But after that day, he no longer saw them as evil or different or less human than he was.

From that day on, Dave never prayed to God for protection or to help him be victorious in battle. Instead, he prayed that God would heal the wounds that he was creating, and he would pray for the families of those he had to kill. His judgmentalism had turned to openness.

As part of the treatment for his alcoholism, Dave decided to frame the German soldier's photo and place it next to a candle. Each day, he lit the candle and said a prayer for that fallen soldier and his wife and two children. I'm sure that he prayed for that family until the day he died. He also did volunteer work at the local veterans' hospital, and he stopped drinking and stayed sober.

Questions for contemplation:

1. Can you recall an incident or period in your life when you were very judgmental? What were you judgmental about? What was happening in your life at the time? How afraid or sad were you?

2. Can you recall an incident or period in your life when you were very open? What was happening in your life at the time? How happy were you?

3. As of today, where do you place yourself on the continuum from judgmentalism to openness?

Unfairness   **Fairness**

Unfairness

The world is not fair. It never has been and never will be. As my friend Alex says, "If the world were fair and we all got what we deserved, I'd be living in some trailer park next to a toxic landfill with a pet hamster as my best friend, and the person living there now might be living in my beautiful home with my beautiful wife."

Actually, Alex is too hard on himself, but he has a point. Sometimes we get what we feel is fair, and sometimes we don't. Good things happen and bad things happen.

Sometimes unfairness gets passed on like a disease. When we've been treated unfairly, we can develop a sense of entitlement; we can feel justified in treating others unfairly. We then use our own difficulties as excuses for acts of greed, exploitation, or neglect. *There have always been poor people, so my giving to a charity won't make any difference. . . . I didn't have it easy when I grew up, and I made it! People should quit whining about how hard they have it and get busy. Life is not fair, so quit asking me for a handout. . . . I can't help you with your problems right now—I've got too many of my own. You're on your own.* We hide behind the unfairness of life rather than work to make the world a little better for everyone.

Sometimes we may use unfairness to manipulate others

into giving us what we want (or believe we deserve). "It's not fair that you're making me stay home and do my homework when all my friends get to go to the concert!" "It's not fair that I got laid off from my job—I've been there for twenty years! Now that I'm out of work, both of you need to drop out of college and work full time so we can pay the mortgage."

Our reptilian brains are wired to tell us that there isn't enough, and that we should do whatever is necessary to get what we lack, even if that means being unfair. But our neo-cortex knows better—that there is a bigger picture, and that we're all in this together.

Fairness

We can't control the world, but we *can* control whether we treat others with fairness or unfairness. We can do our best to be fair and just.

Fairness seeks to balance the needs of all involved and to weigh all elements—not just the ones we care about. Fairness seeks resolutions that are larger than merely what works best for *us*.

Focusing on fairness helps us keep things in perspective. We know that there are always others more deserving than we are, and we remember that the good things that come our way result not only from our own efforts, but also from the hard work of others.

While we can't make the world free of unfairness, we can consciously choose to act fairly. We can acknowledge the needs and interests of everyone involved, not just our own. And when we come face to face with the unfairness of life, we can work to change it, at least a little. As Gandhi said, "Be the change you wish to see in the world."

Fairness is a by-product Principle, the result of bringing together other positive Spiritual Principles such as dignity, respect, justice, tolerance, and integrity to address situations and problems.

Two friends are out for a walk near a lake. They come across an area where someone has overturned a trash can. One friend complains how stupid and unfair it is to make such a mess for someone else to pick up. The other friend quietly bends down and starts picking up the trash. This is practical spirituality and an example of fairness in action.

Heidi's Story

As a young child, Heidi often complained about how rough her life was, and how much more fortunate some of her friends were. True, her parents didn't have a lot of money, but Heidi was healthy and her family was generally loving and supportive.

When Heidi started her senior year in high school, her physics teacher assigned her to sit behind Sara, a beautiful girl who had lost the use of her legs in a skiing accident. Sara spent most of her time in a wheelchair.

At first Heidi was upset at being positioned behind "the girl in the chair." In fact, what bothered Heidi the most was how friendly and pleasant Sara was most of the time. Her niceness really annoyed Heidi.

One day Heidi couldn't stand it anymore. She said to Sara, "Why aren't you angry? You'll never be getting out of that damn chair. Aren't you upset about what happened?"

Sara leaned over and touched Heidi's hand. "Heidi, of course I wish I could walk again. Some nights I cry myself to sleep knowing I won't ever walk again. But when I get stuck in thinking that life isn't fair, I just remember the girl I met in the hospital. She was in a wheelchair, too, but she could hardly move any part of her body. She was learning to communicate by blowing into a tube. I guess I feel pretty lucky next to her."

Heidi just sat quietly; she felt like crying and didn't know why.

Later that day at lunch, Heidi asked Sara if she could sit with her. Sara said, "Sure, have a seat."

The moment Heidi sat down, questions started to roll from her mouth. Sara patiently answered them all, and after twenty minutes, she laughed and said, "Heidi, maybe you need to volunteer at the hospital and see what some folks have to deal with."

A few weeks later, Heidi did just that. She and Sara also became best friends—and Heidi launched a campaign that got Sara elected as homecoming queen.

Questions for contemplation:

1. Is there an issue or situation in your life that you feel is especially unfair? When you think about this situation or issue, how do you feel? Knowing that it's not possible to make life completely fair, what have you done so far to handle this situation or issue—either to make it better or to make it worse? What can you do to make it better that you aren't doing now?

2. Is there an aspect of life *in general* that you feel is especially unfair? Knowing that it's not possible to make life completely fair, what have you done about this aspect of life to make things more fair for at least one other person? What can you do that you aren't doing now?

3. As of right now, where do you place yourself on the continuum from unfairness to fairness?

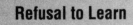

Refusal to Learn   Wisdom

Refusal to Learn

A professor friend told me she was frustrated because many of her students didn't want to learn; instead, they just want information. "They don't do the hard work of thinking; they just want me to be a human version of Google," she said.

Learning is much more than simply acquiring information. Like apples getting transformed into apple pie, information needs to be transformed into knowledge, then knowledge must be transformed into action, and then again into wisdom. This takes place only when the information is integrated into our two spiritual centers, our head and our heart. Studying pushes knowledge into our head; real-world decisions and actions push it into our heart. Only then have we genuinely learned; only then have we moved toward wisdom.

Wisdom contains humility. It understands that it's always incomplete; even as it makes us more human, it leads us back to how little we know and the wonder of the everyday.

Wisdom isn't static; it leads to doing. Knowing and doing together are always more honest—and more valuable—than merely knowing. Wisdom involves relationships, multiple insights, and context—like nearly everything else that's important in life.

A refusal to learn resists all of this. Usually fear is behind this resistance; often pride and ego feed it as well.

Someone who refuses to learn usually thinks, *I don't need to learn about this, because I already know.* But the danger of already knowing is that it can seduce us into a false sense of completion, a false sense of finality. Already knowing is restrictive and contracting, while wisdom is ever-expanding.

When we refuse to learn and explore new ideas, we shut down. We exchange a question mark for a period—or, worse, an exclamation point. We may start to defend the little we know, like gang members defending their own small turf. We may even see other ideas, or other ways of thinking or being, as dangerous. We may then want others to be submissive to our ideas and information. We may even choose to distort information in order to use it as a weapon to gain power.

Another way we refuse to learn is by seeing ourselves as not smart enough. We may pretend to be naïve or thick headed as a way to avoid having to learn the lessons that life puts before us. Adopting this attitude diminishes our conscience and subtly gives us permission to pursue sensations of pleasure or power.

Wisdom

Wisdom is not a state of accumulated knowledge, but a by-product of searching for meaning and a willingness to be open to the ongoing lessons of life.

I asked an older gentleman whom I respect how he got to be so wise. His answer: "I've mainly kept my eyes open and my mouth shut—and I've been blessed by my Higher Power with the gift of curiosity."

The major ingredient of wisdom is humility. Wisdom accepts its own limits. It knows the fragile balance we walk between ego and integrity, between instinct and humanity, between good deeds and hurtful deeds. It understands and accepts the incompleteness of our condition and the challenge of seeing life through the eyes of a beginner.

Wisdom is not a static state of being or achievement, for it can disappear in a moment of pride. A person of wisdom understands that any positive Spiritual Principle is purer and closer to the Divine than they are. They also recognize that they must always be willing to surrender any parts of their ego that get in the way of those Principles.

Wisdom avoids stagnation and knows that the Divine is fluid—and that it must be, to seep through the large and small wounds of our heart in order to heal.

Over time, wisdom weaves positive Spiritual Principles into a value system, and then turns that value system into a functioning conscience. When this happens, we end up with another source of wisdom through conscious contact—the collective voices of positive Spiritual Principles echoing throughout our being and guiding our behaviors. This takes time, and it is partly why we equate wisdom with age. Thus when we meet a wise young person, we call him an "old soul" or "wise beyond her years," because developing conscious, intimate relationships with all the positive Spiritual Principles is the work of a lifetime.

Aaron's Story

Aaron grew up with an abusive father and an alcoholic mother. But Aaron had a wonderful, wise grandfather who understood that Aaron's parents were grappling with their own demons, but who also loved his grandson and realized his safety was at risk. On weekends Grandpa Mike would pick up Aaron, and they would go to Grandpa Mike's cabin in the woods. Grandpa Mike taught Aaron all about nature and how to survive in the forest. Grandpa Mike had been a Green Beret in Vietnam and had lived alone in the jungle for months at a time.

One day when Aaron was eight, Grandpa Mike came by to pick him up and found that he had a black eye and an arm in a sling. When Grandpa Mike asked what had happened to him, Aaron said, in a small voice, "I fell down the stairs." But Grandpa Mike had been paying close attention to Aaron's "accidents" over time and had talked to his son about his concerns to no avail. He became convinced that his son and his wife were not capable of learning from their mistakes, and despite the love and concern he felt toward his own son, he believed it was time to take action.

That Sunday night, as Grandpa Mike drove Aaron home, he asked, "Would you like to live with me?" Immediately Aaron said, "Yes."

Grandpa Mike had been waiting for this day, and he'd prepared a plan that was respectful to Aaron's parents, yet would keep his grandson out of harm. Instead of simply dropping off Aaron that night, he sat down with Aaron's mother and father and showed them the pictures he had taken of Aaron's bruises, black eyes, and cuts over the past several months. He said, "Aaron wants to live with me. I'd like that, too. I can provide him with a safe home where no one beats or hurts him. We can pack his suitcase and he can come with me tonight, and you can sign over legal custody once I get you the proper forms. You'll be able to see Aaron often, provided I'm there to observe. Your other option is to keep Aaron here. If you do that, I'll show these photos to Child Protection tomorrow morning. I have no idea how much they'll let you see Aaron once they take him away from you."

Aaron's parents sat silently for several seconds, looking at the photos and at Grandpa Mike. Then Mike's son got up, left the room, and returned a minute later carrying Aaron's suitcase.

Questions for contemplation:

1. Are there any issues or situations that you react to by refusing to learn from them? What emotions can you feel behind this refusal? Next time you're tempted to resist

learning, can you stay with this emotion long enough to let your resistance soften, then think about what positive Spiritual Principles may help?

2. In what places, situations, or people do you routinely find wisdom and guidance?

3. As of right now, where do you place yourself on the continuum from "refusal to learn" to wisdom?

Willfulness	Willingness

Willfulness

Each of us has been given a will, a source of personal energy that is ours and ours alone. This energy gives us a sense of power and uniqueness, as well as the ability and responsibility to make choices. Willfulness is a refusal to offer up this personal energy for the betterment of others through the expression of positive Spiritual Principles. It often goes hand in hand with selfishness, which only increases its resolve.

A friend calls and asks to borrow your car, which you're not using for the day. His is in the shop, he explains, and money is tight. If you help out, he could save the cost of renting a car for the day. But you say no, because you don't like the idea of someone else driving your car. That's willfulness in action.

Or maybe you've been feeling run down for a couple of weeks. Your partner asks you to see a doctor because he's worried about your health. You respond angrily, "I'm okay! I'll see a doctor when I want to see doctor, not just because you're worried." Willfulness puts distance between us and whatever thing, person, or activity we're being willful about. When we become willful, we turn away from positive Spiritual Principles and the Divine, and turn toward instinct and ego. If we stay willful, over time we become rigid and closed-minded. We will push away anyone different from us and any idea different from our own. We then hide in negative spiritual principles like cynicism, skepticism, arrogance, and self-righteousness, seeking refuge from that which challenges and scares us. Willfulness feeds the "reptile" within.

Willingness

Willingness is a form of surrender, a recognition of our shared humanity, and the redirection of our will to benefit others. We see this most clearly in people who choose to put themselves in harm's way in order to serve and protect others, such as police officers, firefighters, and soldiers. But willingness is also behind any form of selfless service, from shoveling an elderly neighbor's sidewalk to helping your daughter's Girl Scout troop sell cookies at the mall.

Willingness always involves vulnerability, which is not something to be feared, but is a gateway to spiritual growth. Willingness and vulnerability both offer us many benefits — closer relationships, deeper commitments, and the opening up of new worlds.

An old friend's wife wanted him to learn to dance, but he became willful and refused, mainly because he hated the thought of being a beginner in a dance class. Over time, however, he was able to transform his willfulness into willingness. He and his wife took the class, and they now go dancing every Saturday.

Twelve Step meetings begin with everyone expressing a willingness to admit their imperfections. Then they are all welcomed for it. "Hi, my name is Pete and I'm an alcoholic." Everyone greets him: "Hi, Pete!" "Hi, I'm Stella and I'm a coke addict." Everyone responds: "Hi, Stella!" Each willing admission of imperfection is immediately followed by others' willingness to accept the person for who he or she is.

Willingness gets created in those moments when we suspend judgments. It allows us to see the many worlds layered and woven around our own. Becoming willing is a blessing, an act of courage, and a personal achievement.

Daniel's Story

Daniel had always been stubborn, even as a child. His parents worked hard to instill in this strong-willed child a variety of healthy values. For example, they had a rule: what is served is what you eat. One night when Daniel was eight, he sat at the table until ten o'clock because he didn't want to eat the liver and lemon pie that his mother had served him.

Daniel's will also had a positive aspect. In high school, he attached his will to perseverance and striving for excellence, and he became a straight-A student and the city's all-star quarterback, earning him a scholarship to a good college.

But when he went away to college, Daniel started to change, and his fame started to inflate his ego. He had to be in control and became self-righteous, arrogant, and cocky. He always got what he wanted and believed it would always be that way.

Sophomore year was a tough year for Daniel. He received a knee injury that ended his football career, and shortly after that, his girlfriend left him for the new quarterback. Daniel turned his pain into a bitterness that continued until he met Christy, who was to become his wife.

Daniel was madly in love with her. He was determined that they would have a good life. After college, he worked hard and became successful, and some of his old willfulness returned. He became controlling again. He started correcting Christy about everything. The more successful Daniel became, the less room there was for Christy and her thoughts, wants, and desires. Daniel thought he knew what was best for them.

One day, Daniel came home from work to find Christy with a suitcase packed. She sat Daniel down and very lovingly and compassionately told him that she was moving out because she couldn't stand his having to be right about everything. She was crying as she told him that she wanted to love him, but she couldn't breathe in the relationship anymore.

It was then that Daniel's willfulness changed to willingness. He didn't want to lose her and begged her for a second chance. She agreed, but only if he would get counseling.

Daniel was a great client. He took his counseling seriously and reattached his will to perseverance, but also to other principles, like compassion, empathy, and humility. Humility allowed him to feel the sadness of his football injury and the loss of his old girlfriend, and to see that fame and glory were shallow friends. It helped him accept that all of us are vulnerable and being right and self-righteous were just his ways of trying to hold on to fame and glory.

He stopped trying to make everything go his way and worked just to be a good man, a good husband, and a good citizen. He learned to make room for Christy, and her love for him blossomed again. As Daniel explained, "The more I'm willing to see my flaws, the more humble I become, for I really see how much I need others—their ideas, care, friendship, and love."

Questions for contemplation:

1. When do you tend to become most willful—in what situations and with what people? What negative emotion—fear, sadness, a sense of powerlessness, and so on—most makes you want to be willful?

2. Think back to a time in your life when your willingness enabled you to take a risk and change a behavior, an attitude, or your situation. What were the results of that change? Now think about a time when your willingness enabled you to give significant help to someone else. How did your willingness change *their* life?

3. As of right now, where do you place yourself on the continuum from willfulness to willingness?

Perfectionism   Excellence

Perfectionism

When we demand perfection, we only frustrate ourselves and hurt others.

Perfectionism is a lie. It would have us believe that we can arrive at a place or achieve a level of skill, competence, or thought where we are not flawed. This will never happen. Being half animal and half spiritual, we can't be either one perfectly. This is why excellence is a worthy goal, and perfection is an impossible one.

Perfectionism feeds the natural narcissism that is part of our me-centered instinctual side by pushing aside acceptance and humility.

People who push themselves to be perfect become ashamed of their flaws, and these flaws then can haunt them. I once had a client who was a perfectionist about her body. She was a beautiful woman in her early sixties. She hated herself because she didn't look forty or thirty, and she constantly berated herself. *I'm all used up; all my good years are behind me. I hate the way I look and what life has done to my body.*

It took time, but eventually she saw that she was doing far more damage to herself than age ever did. Eventually, she accepted herself for who she was: a normal, flawed, and aging human being.

A wonderful proverb says, "A beautiful thing is never perfect." Our imperfections are natural parts of all of us—and natural parts of human life. They are also gifts given to us to help us see a need for each other, to help us support one another, and to help us develop deeper relationships with positive Spiritual Principles.

Gandhi wrote, "My imperfections and failures are as much a blessing from God as my successes and my talents, and I lay them both at his feet." Emerson made a similar observation: "There is a crack in everything God has made." The Amish, excellent furniture makers, always put a mistake or flaw in each piece they create because of their belief that the only perfect thing is God.

Excellence

Excellence is striving to do our best and to be of greatest service. It is simultaneously an attitude and a goal.

Armand recently described his two brothers to some friends: "Keith is an okay brother. He runs his own company and has little time for anyone else. When he comes to family gatherings, he often comes late and has to leave early—but he's always friendly and pleasant to everyone. Daniel has Down syndrome and an IQ between sixty-five and seventy, but he is an excellent brother, the best you could ask for. He always calls me on my birthday; he always asks about Keith; he's very proud of both of his brothers. He worked his tail off so he could live with three other guys and a counselor in a group home, because he didn't want to be a burden to Mom and Dad as they got older. He's been a loyal employee at a fast food restaurant for the past four years. He sweeps and mops the floor and greets all the customers. He shows up at Mom and Dad's house every Saturday with flowers for Mom, and he's always ready to be a "go-fer" for Dad for any projects he may have. He always has a kind word for everyone. Because of the heart defects that are part of his condition, he most likely won't have a long life. I pray that I can be half the man he is."

Bertha's Story

About ten years ago, I had a client named Bertha, who told me this story:

"I've been chasing perfection all my life, and what did it get me? An ulcer and a gambling problem. I grew up being the top student in my class. But that wasn't good enough for me. I wanted to be number one in the school district. When I ended up being number two in my senior year of high school, I cried for three days straight.

"I went to church regularly, and what I heard our minister say was that I was made in God's image, and God was perfect, so I should work to be perfect, too. I liked the thought that if I could achieve perfection, I would please God.

"In college I had the highest GPA in my class. But I also developed an ulcer and was sent to counseling. I went twice, but then stopped—I thought the counselor was trying to encourage me to be weak.

"After college, I went on to earn a master's degree and a Ph.D. Soon after that, I became a researcher.

"I had boyfriends on and off, but the relationships wouldn't last long. I'd quickly see all of the ways each of the guys could improve themselves, and then I would work to change them. They would get angry and tire of me, and I would sink myself into my work again.

"When I was twenty-five, a girlfriend wanted to go to a casino for her birthday. Six of us went, and we had a wonderful evening. I'd never been inside a casino before, and I immediately found it mesmerizing. I especially loved the slot machines. There was something both very exciting and very peaceful about them.

That first night, I hit a jackpot and won two hundred dollars. I felt like I was in heaven. This place had everything a girl could ask for: friendly atmosphere, endless fun, free money—but mostly the peaceful trance of the slot machines, quieting those pushy voices inside of me.

"Within a month, I was going out to the casino at least once a week. I deliberately played only the penny slot machines. Still, I would usually lose a couple of hundred dollars a trip. I was given a player's card and earned points and rewards. After about a year, I got to stay free on weekends and sometimes gambled for twenty-four hours at a time. I loved the trance and how it quieted the voices of perfection in my head—blissful silence.

"One weekend I lost two thousand dollars. I had maxed out all my credit cards, and my ulcer started acting up badly. I ended up in the hospital.

"My parents and the hospital social worker convinced me to go to treatment. That's how I ended up here."

Bertha was officially treated for a gambling addiction, but she also had a serious need to be perfect that helped set her up for addiction. To her credit, she stopped gambling, attended Gamblers Anonymous, and stopped demanding impossible things of herself and others. Evidently, she did well enough that she could date and not have to fix others. She's been happily married for several years now.

Questions for contemplation:

1. When have you tried to be perfect—or had someone else try to make you perfect? What was the result of that attempt at perfection? When have you hurt others by trying to make *them* perfect? What were the results of your efforts?

2. Is there one thing you would most like to excel at? What is it? What are the initial steps you can take toward

achieving that excellence? Can you take those steps now, or very soon?

3. As of today, where do you place yourself on the continuum from perfectionism to excellence?

Cynicism

Cynicism is looking at everything and seeing only (or mostly) its negative qualities. Cynicism distrusts the integrity and motives of others, and it can take a diamond and turn it back into coal.

Robin inherits $400,000; she cynically complains to her friend about the tax problems she will have and the relatives who will come out of the woodwork.

After a year of physical therapy, Emilio fully recovers from his stroke. His cynical cousin tells him, "You know, you have a 47 percent chance of having another stroke."

Cynicism arises from fear, a sense of powerlessness, and a desire to be in control. The cynic is afraid to trust, afraid to be vulnerable—yet cynics often see themselves as better or smarter or more realistic than others. Although cynics see others as motivated primarily by selfishness, this is mostly a projection of their own selfishness.

Cynics try to protect themselves by believing the worst about people or events. Cynicism is thus a subtle form of aggression. Cynics hope to convince others to submit to their negativity—or, at least, to accept that negativity as a form of wisdom. Cynicism is a subtle form of another "-ism," narcissism, because it is ultimately about self-protection.

Gratitude

Gratitude is an acceptance of, and a rejoicing in, what is inside and around us. It is an acknowledgment that love and hope exist and can be found in the everyday.

Gratitude looks beyond surface events to appreciate connections, beauty, and mystery. It is the wholehearted embracing of the here and now, a belief that the present moment is enough.

Gratitude offers us freedom from worry, regret, and trepidation about the future. It also offers us protection against fear, cynicism, and negativity. Gratitude effectively counters shame, pushes fears away, and frees up energy to be redirected toward learning and finding meaning.

Gratitude allows us to experience the moment and allows the moment to be enough.

Jason's Story

Ten years ago, when he was twenty-seven, Jason sat in a doctor's office, feeling angry and cynical. He had just been told that he had cancer and would need an operation to remove a tumor. Then he would need to undergo a series of chemo treatments for several months. Jason was more afraid than he had ever been before.

His was not an aggressive form of cancer, but it was still dangerous and needed to be treated. Jason had always been a bit of a cynic, but his illness became his excuse to wallow in cynicism. He complained to friends, relatives, neighbors, and anyone who would listen about the frailty of the human body, the limitations of medical care, the confusion of dealing with his health insurance company, and the limited life spans of human beings.

Jason had his operation and his chemo, and both went well. He recovered fully from the cancer but not from his cynicism.

Eight months after the operation, he was pushing his grocery cart down the supermarket bakery aisle when a woman acciden- tally pushed her cart into his. People are jerks, *a voice inside him complained.* "Why don't you watch where you are going?" *he half-shouted.*

Jason's anger turned to embarrassment a moment later when he realized that the woman was one of the nurses in the hos- pital who had cared for him after his operation. He quickly apol- ogized, and so did she. "I guess I'm better with IVs than I am with shopping carts," *she said. They began talking, and after ten minutes, when she turned to leave, Jason reached past his cyni- cism and asked her,* "Would you like to go to lunch sometime?"

"Sure," she said, smiling. "That sounds good."

She and Jason began dating and eventually married. His cynicism gradually dissolved as their love grew.

When I met Jason, he was in his thirties. He lived each day with great gratitude. With awe in his voice, he told me the story of his cancer, the encounter in the grocery store, and his marriage. "I wouldn't have found her without the cancer," *he said.* "If we hadn't met in the store the way we did, carts crashing— well, who knows? Since that day I've been open to the mysteries of life and the gifts life brings."

Questions for contemplation:

1. Can you recall some moments or periods in your life when you sought the false protection of cynicism? Can you identify the fear, the sadness, or the feelings of powerlessness that lay beneath the cynicism?

2. What things do you have in your life right now that you are most grateful for? Why?

3. As of right now, where do you place yourself on the continuum from cynicism to gratitude?

Chaos	Discipline

Chaos

In Greek mythology, Chaos was the dark abyss from which everything came—a beginning point, not a place of refuge.

In everyday life, however, chaos is that groundless, rudderless state that results from endlessly (and mindlessly) chasing after things—sensations, thrills, experiences, objects, people, prestige, power, or even comfort. In a life ruled by chaos, busyness means everything. But chaos makes it hard to put a coherent life together, for our energies never coalesce to push us in a purposeful, disciplined direction.

Chaos can be very seductive. We can use its ongoing sense of urgency—the strong desire to run after and acquire the next thing—to avoid the responsibilities of finding meaning and putting together a life. People who fear responsibility sometimes use a lifestyle of chaos to help them avoid responsibility—and to block out their fear of it.

The noise of chaos often drowns out our internal voices of meaning and connection. Keeping busy can become a goal in itself, rather than a way to harness our energies in service of others and positive Spiritual Principles.

But a life of chaos cannot be sustained indefinitely. Eventually, our energies run down, the whirling slows, and the fears, pains, and hollowness we have been trying to avoid are right in front of us.

When a client who had lived a life of chaos first came to me, he said, "For over fifty years, I've been getting up early each day, running off, and chasing things just for the sake of chasing them. But nothing means anything. I can't tell you one person I'm really close to, including my wife and three children. I love them, but if I stop and think about it, I know nothing of who they are—what their favorite colors are, what brings them joy, or even if they like me. Hell, I don't even know if I like them." That admission was his first step in slowing down enough to start to recover from chaos.

Discipline

Discipline enables us to create and stay within a structure, to direct our energies toward specific goals, and to stay connected to positive Spiritual Principles. Discipline is a form of love.

Our self-centeredness can make us distrustful of discipline. We may feel like discipline will take something from us or cheat us out of something. Indeed, discipline goes against our instinctual side, which mostly wants to be fed well, taken care of, waited on, and provided with pleasure, comfort, and gratification. Discipline is taking responsibility, then training and directing one's energies through positive Spiritual Principles.

Through discipline, we domesticate our instinctual side without breaking its spirit. We protect ourselves from our own impulsiveness and keep our drives for pleasure, power, and meaning in balance.

Discipline—like tolerance, patience, and concentration—changes our relationship with time, slowing down difficult and emotionally charged moments, so we act less from impulse and more from positive Spiritual Principles.

Discipline requires us to create a healthy relationship with the word *no*. *No* is not just a word; it is a vehicle to freedom. *Yes* speaks to the things we embrace and bring closer to us; *no* is about things we have decided to pass by. *No* often requires extra thought. Discipline requires us to look at our choices and determine whether they will benefit or harm our connection with positive Spiritual Principles. We need to say no to people, places, and events that weaken our connection with these Principles, even when saying yes might seem fun, enjoyable, exciting, or comforting.

Discipline tells us to say no to the frustration we feel as we watch our children struggle with a simple math problem. We may want to give them the answer to end our frustration, but discipline tells us to wait silently and give them time so they can learn. Discipline tells us to say no to the desire to flirt with our neighbor (and to say yes to our desire to flirt with our partner). Discipline tells us not to answer the phone when our best friend calls, because we're having dinner with our family and our kids are telling us about their day.

Hagar's Story

Hagar was a Cherokee elder who consistently lived a life of discipline. Hagar dedicated himself to his job at a food processing plant and to serving his community. He carefully carved out time each week to volunteer on the reservation, assisting people who were sick and dying. He also went to all his son's high school football games. He did not drink or smoke, except for his prayer pipe. He also served as a mentor to my friend Andy.

Andy lived a fairly chaotic life until he met Hagar. Hagar took Andy under his wing and pushed him to see his energy as a gift to be used for the betterment of others and himself. Hagar sometimes took Andy deep into the woods and made him sit very quietly for long periods of time. The longer and more quietly they would sit, the safer the forest animals would feel. Then the forest would come alive with movement and sounds. Hagar had Andy continue his discipline of sitting and being quiet until one day a deer walked by them no more than ten feet away.

Once Andy had disciplined himself to the point of being still, Hagar encouraged him to start helping and giving to others. Andy started volunteering at the local food pantry one day a week and reading to a blind man at a local nursing home.

As Hagar told Andy, "To have an undisciplined life is to have a life with no center, a life with no purpose, a body with no heart. It is through the quieting of ourselves that we learn to hear the voice of the Great Creator. It is through the disciplining of our energies that we can offer ourselves up to be of service to the Great Creator."

Questions for contemplation:

1. Think back to a time when you used chaos as a way to avoid a relationship or a responsibility. What did you tell yourself in order to keep the noise going? What were the results of this time of chaos?

2. Write down three aspects of your life that could be improved by practicing discipline. What would more discipline look like in each case? How would things be different once you applied that discipline for a few weeks or months?

3. As of right now, where do you place yourself on the continuum from chaos to discipline?

Separateness	Unity

Separateness

Separateness is a refusal to see the interconnectedness of all things, taking refuge in the pieces instead of celebrating the beauty of the whole.

Separateness tells us that we don't need others—that, in fact, they are burdens or pose a threat. This is a classic reptilian brain response, because reptiles don't need others. But we humans do. It is only in relationships with others and self that we develop our morality.

We may use separateness to preserve a delusion, so that the story we tell ourselves never gets challenged by others in the court of social interactions. We then get to be the king or queen in a kingdom of one.

Separateness, like most other negative spiritual principles, has its roots in fear. Our reptilian brain seeks separateness (or dominance) when it's afraid. Think of those intense fights we've all had with our spouses, our parents, or other people who are important to us, in which we say (or want to say), "Just leave me alone! I don't need this. I don't need you. Just let me be!" Then we fold our arms or place our hands on our hips, signaling the other person to back away.

Often we stay separate by aligning with others, but only those others who see the world exactly as we do. We and our allies then separate our group from the rest of humanity. This may look and feel like unity or loyalty, but it is simply a shared separateness, a kind of group narcissism.

Unity

Unity asks that we see the connectedness that envelops us and accept our responsibility to share Spirit with each other.

Unity is a sacred act of free will. It enables us to see that collective common welfare is only achieved when each of us contributes to it—and when we place the needs of the Divine ahead of the desires and wants of individuals, including ourselves.

Becky's Story

Many years ago, I had the privilege of listening to Becky tell her story of spiritual recovery. She had suffered at the hands of abusive parents, and then was exploited by a minister who used her vulnerability for his own sexual satisfaction. Because of this, by the time she was an adult, she trusted no one.

Becky protected herself by becoming invisible. She became an expert at being unseen. She said little (just enough to get by), challenged people as little as possible, and had no relationships other than the simplest and most basic ones. Becky's main way of dealing with what life had given her was through her drug addiction.

Becky went through three unsuccessful treatments for her addiction. Each time, she managed to stay aloof and avoided changing her perspective or confronting her past. Her internal dialogue was mainly about why others were dangerous and not to be trusted. Each time, she was able to evade her counselor's efforts to connect with her and help her with her illness.

In her fourth treatment, however, she was more fortunate.

She got a counselor who refused to not see her. As in past treatments, she spent as much time as possible alone, drawing. After a week and half, her counselor came to her room and demanded to see the drawings she had made while sitting tucked away from the others.

Although Becky had separated herself from people and from all close human relationships, she had kept open her connection to the Divine through her relationship with paper and pencil. Her drawings were horribly beautiful. Their honesty was shocking, their content deeply revealing.

Becky's counselor had her pin all of her drawings on the walls of the treatment center's community room. She sat in the center of the room and required Becky to sit beside her. Neither said a word as the other patients, counselors, and the director of the center viewed Becky's drawings.

The black-and-white drawings were mainly graphic depictions of a faceless girl being sexually violated. They brought most of the people who viewed them to tears.

That day was Becky's first day of being noticed and heard in a safe, caring way. Becky saw the profound effect her drawings had on everyone who viewed them.

Becky's edge and separateness began to soften when the director of the program brought her flowers and said through her tears, "I'm truly sorry for your suffering. Thank you for surviving. You are a true artist." Becky reached out and took her counselor's hand.

For the next four evenings, Becky drew at a fevered pace, working to expel the shards of evil that had been embedded in her soul. She redrew all of the pictures, and many more. This time though, the girl was not faceless; Becky's face was on each drawing. She had fought back evil with paper and a pencil.

On the morning of the fifth day, she asked her counselor for colored pencils. She said simply, "It's done. I'd like to draw a picture of the flowers now, before they fade away."

In the months that followed, Becky found her way back to unity and humanity. Today, Becky is drug free, does volunteer work with abused girls, and is a professional wildflower artist.

Questions for contemplation:

1. When you're under stress, in what ways do you separate yourself from others in order to feel safe? What would happen if you acknowledged this impulse and told people about it? What are some things you could do to stay connected instead?

2. When you feel like separating yourself from others, what emotions are usually present? Fear? Anger? Sadness?

3. As of right now, where do you place yourself on the continuum from separateness to unity?

Rugged Individualism	Relationship

Rugged Individualism

Rugged individualism is not a combination of self-confidence and self-reliance, which are both positive human qualities. Instead, it is the erroneous belief that it is somehow possible to live a full human life without the help of other people — or the Divine.

Rugged individualism refuses to acknowledge that humans are spiritual and social creatures. Thus it is a form of denial, an attempt to ignore part of our humanity.

Rugged individualism comes straight out of our reptilian brains. Indeed, all reptiles live their lives as rugged individuals, and the reptilian world is entirely unaware of caring.

Often, under the hard crust of rugged individualism is a person who has been deeply hurt, or who was never adequately cared for or loved. As a counselor for forty-plus years, I've learned that people who seek refuge in rugged individualism often have some of the saddest stories of abuse and neglect. Their rugged individualism is an adaptation, a way to feel safe in a world that they have experienced as cold, unloving, and painful.

Rugged individualism is different from separateness in that there is not only a desire to stay disconnected, but a core belief that others are not needed.

The biggest danger in rugged individualism is the loss of feedback from others. Without close relationships, we have no checks or balances to counteract our reptilian brains, which can slowly take over our feelings and thoughts. Over time, our pain can harden and eventually turn into hate.

Relationship

We humans live our lives in the context of relationships. They are what make us human; indeed, the depth of our relationships is what creates a rich and meaningful life. Through relationships, we not only learn that "we" is more important than "me," but that "we" supports and develops a spiritually healthy "me," countering our natural self-centeredness. It is also through relationships that we get a meaningful and accurate picture of ourselves.

Relationships challenge us to care, to act, to help, to understand, to empathize, and to change. They push us to see what we have in common with others and to act on that commonality.

We can use relationships to build places of sanctuary. Within these safe relationships, we can more readily explore other positive Spiritual Principles, such as empathy, compassion, and love. Indeed, since morality only develops within the context of relationships, caring and safe relationships are necessary if we are to find and develop our moral compass.

LuAnne's Story

LuAnne was eighty-eight years old. Her husband, Marlon, had died four years before, at the age of eighty-eight. LuAnne lived in the same two-story home that she and Marlon had bought when they first married, and she made it clear to both her middle-aged children that she had no intention of moving—ever.

"This is my home," she told them. "It's not some anonymous

apartment. Marlon and I raised a family here. You see the deck out back? Marlon built it himself."

A year after their father's death, both of LuAnne's children began suggesting to her that she look into an assisted-living complex. "Mom," her son, Soren, said, "we worry about you being all alone, and going up and down those stairs. What if something happens to you? It's not like we live in town and can check in on you every day."

"Fifty miles away is close enough," LuAnne insisted. "I've been getting along just fine with you driving in once a week and taking me on errands. I'm very happy right where I am."

Eventually Soren gave up trying to change his mother's mind. But LuAnne's daughter, Belinda, persisted. "Mom, it's not just about where you live. It's also about being all by yourself. Soren and I would be happy to have someone come in for a couple of hours a day. They can cook for you, do your laundry, help you out around the house."

"Absolutely not," LuAnne said firmly. "This is my home, not some retirement community. I'm perfectly happy with the way I cook, and I like the way I do my laundry. When I want someone to cook for me, I pick up the phone and order Chinese delivery."

"How about just having someone come in once a week?"

"Lindy, what part of no don't you understand? I thought I raised you to listen when people speak to you."

"Mom, you're impossible."

"Look, honey, I know you want what's best for me. But what makes me happy is to live in my own home. I'd be miserable in some apartment complex full of people as old and as cranky as I am." Eventually both children stopped trying to change their mother's mind. Then, one morning, Belinda got a call on her cell phone.

"Lindy, it's Soren. Have you talked to Mom recently? I got her voice mail when I called yesterday, and I got it again this morning."

"Same deal for me. What do you think?"

"I think one of us needs to drive over and take a look. Can you go? I'm on my way to my daughter's flute recital."

"Soren, I flew to Montreal this morning on business, remember?"

"Crap. Okay, I'm on my way to Mom's. Man, this sucks."

An hour later, Soren found his mother at the foot of her stairs, crying and moaning, her body twisted up. He dialed 911, then got her a cup of water and helped her drink. "My hip," she gasped. "I think I broke my hip."

LuAnne had broken her hip. She had also managed to avoid having to move to assisted living. She went straight from the hospital to a nursing home, where she spent the remaining two years of her life.

Questions for contemplation:

1. Think of a time or situation in which you chose to go it alone rather than ask for help. What emotions did you feel at the time? What made you decide not to ask for help? What were your thoughts about others?

2. Think of someone you know whom you'd like to get closer to. What specific things might you do to begin to build or deepen that relationship?

3. As of right now, where do you place yourself on the continuum from rugged individualism to relationship?

Lies	Truth

Lies

Truth asks us to be responsible to others and ourselves; lies are an avoidance of these responsibilities. They are forms of self-protection that ultimately isolate us, erode our relationships with others, and encourage further lies.

Whether we lie to others, to ourselves, or both, lies put distance between us and others—and between us and positive Spiritual Principles. Lies encourage us to be lazy, and they tend to make us rigid and self-absorbed. They can also create a cage that traps us.

Most lies are based in fear. As a compulsive liar once told me, "Whenever I'm with someone and I feel that faint flicker of fear inside, out comes a lie. I still remember when it worked for the first time. My father was angry and asked me if I had taken a tool of his, which I had. I was scared, but I looked him directly in the eye and told him no. I saw him buy the lie, and I felt great relief; I was safe. Whenever I face a situation where I don't know what to do, I lie. When my lies are accepted, it brings me a brief sense of relief and safety."

Although some lies can seem clever and devious, the impulse to lie comes from our reptilian brain, as part of the fight, flee, or freeze response. When our reptilian brain gets frightened, it may urge us to lie as a way to avoid potentially painful conflicts, emotions, or consequences.

Truth

There are three different levels or types of truth: (1) my truth, (2) a truth, and (3) The Truth.

A personal truth, *my truth*, is a way we see the world and believe it to be. This is the lowest level of truth. These individual truths are often misguided, full of ego and personal agendas. Yet they are real and valid for us, so we must speak these truths, as incomplete and as questionable as they may be—but we need to *see* them as incomplete.

Indeed, there is beauty in their incompleteness, for it is in their incompleteness that we find a need for others. If I share my incomplete truth with others and others do the same with me—and if we listen to and hear each other—then together we may realize or discover *a truth*.

A truth is the kind of truth we find when we put ego aside and open ourselves to learning, to new and different ideas, and to others' wisdom. We most often come across *a truth* in the context of authentic, caring relationships. In self-help groups, worship services, classrooms, and other such places and events, relationships help us discover truths that hold more Spirit and love than our own personal truths.

When we discover *a truth*, we need to be willing to let go of *my truth*, embrace this higher truth, and make it part of us. In fact, self-improvement is a process of continually exchanging our personal truths for higher truths, and then acting from these higher truths. In doing so, we add more care, knowledge, and love to the world.

Then there is also *The Truth*—something that none of us can know. As incomplete beings—half animal, half spiritual—we humans can never know *The Truth*, only pieces of it. Positive Spiritual Principles are examples of these pieces.

If you meet someone who claims to know *The Truth*, turn and run away as fast as you can. Pretending that *my truth* is

The Truth is dangerous at best, evil at worst. Those who claim to know *The Truth* are almost always looking for power and a way to control others. They want us to submit to them and *their truth*; if we do this well enough and completely enough, we become one of the anointed "knowers," with special rights and privileges. We get to search for others to dominate or to see as wrong or as less than us. Racism, ageism, sexism, and fundamentalism are all forms of *my truth* masquerading as *The Truth*. This is one of the most common ways in which evil is created.

We need not defend or fight for truth, because truth already has far more power than any of us. When we fight for truth, we weaken it by bringing it down to our level. We are to stand with truth, not fight for it.

Spencer's Story

Colin was a very successful man, a man of means and power. As he framed it, what he believed about right and wrong was The Truth, and he had little time, energy, patience, or empathy for anyone who didn't believe as he did, who didn't follow that same Truth.

He taught this Truth to his son, Spencer, and reinforced its absolute correctness by beating Spencer whenever the boy questioned it or failed to follow it to the letter.

Spencer became my client when he was twenty-eight. He had no self-confidence; it had been beaten out of him. He came to me to learn to trust himself and to heal from and grow beyond the pain of the abuse he suffered while growing up.

As part of his counseling, Spencer decided to arrange a session with his father, to confront him and get some answers. Colin agreed to the session and told me that he would help his son in any way possible.

At the session, Spencer began by calmly saying to his father that he wanted to understand why Colin had treated him so roughly as a child. He also asked for an apology for the beatings, especially one in which Spencer's arm had been broken.

Colin quickly went into a rage. "It was my duty!" he shouted. "You had a rebellious spirit and I had to break it. You wouldn't accept The Truth. You mocked it and questioned it! If I hadn't beaten you, you would have lived a life of sin and darkness. You were weak—and you still are. I beat you out of love, so that you would follow The Truth instead of your own weakness."

Spencer calmly held his ground and refused to accept the shame his father was trying to inject into him. The calmer he stayed, the more enraged Colin became. Then Spencer said, "What you call weakness, I call curiosity and intelligence. All I'm asking of you, Dad, is to admit that what you did was wrong, that it wasn't okay to break your child's arm in the name of teaching him a lesson."

Colin stared at Spencer. Finally he said, "You'll go to hell for the way you've dishonored and talked to me today. I disown you as my son." And he got up and walked out the door.

Colin kept his promise; a few weeks later he did formally disown his son. Yet Spencer was comforted by what happened that day, for he confirmed something he had long suspected: that his father was an angry, abusive man, not the guardian of The Truth that he claimed to be.

The last time I saw Spencer, he had made a good life with his wife and their two sons. His father went to his grave never having met Spencer's family.

Questions for contemplation:

1. Think of the biggest lie you ever told, either to others or to yourself. Why did you tell it? What were you afraid would happen if you told the truth? What happened as a result of your telling that lie?

2. Think of a personal truth that is no longer working well for you. Do you know someone who can examine that personal truth with you—without judging you or trying to get you to replace it with *their* truth? Can you meet with them to discuss this soon?

3. As of right now, where do you place yourself on the continuum from lies to truth?

Inequality

We're all different when it comes to our physical character-istics, emotional makeup, financial situations, and so on. But when it comes to our inherent value as human beings, or the degree to which we deserve love and respect, all of us are equal.

When we believe in or practice inequality, we say to others, "I am better, more important, or more deserving than you." Or, in the much more rare form of inequality known as false humil-ity, we believe or tell others that we are inherently *less* worthy than they are. Either way, this can easily create a domino effect that encourages us to embrace other negative spiritual princi-ples, such as greed, indifference, injustice, apathy, entitlement, and arrogance.

Inequality occurs on both a large scale, where it creates social inequality, and a personal level, where it creates frustra-tion, anger, ill will, and outright rebellion.

Inequality is a way we seek to protect ourselves by placing ourselves in a superior position. Once one has fallen in love with the sensations of power this brings, inequality will easily be justified. Inequality works to preserve the *me* over the *we*. This is the most dangerous element of inequality. Inequality creates separateness and marginalizes others.

Equality

Equality comes from an awareness that all of us share the same purposes in life: to place principles before personalities, to help one another, to make a place at the table for everyone, and to live according to positive Spiritual Principles.

Equality counters the natural selfishness that is part of being human. It helps us to deflate our ego and to remember that we exist not just to get ahead, but to sacrifice so we all can get ahead together. Equality helps us stay connected to each other.

Canowicakte's Story

A century ago, Canowicakte was the leader of his band of Lakota in the plains of southern Minnesota. He was known as a good leader and a kind, wise man. Part of his job, as he saw it, was to ensure that all members of the band viewed each other—and him—as equals, though with different talents.

This was a time of great hardship and poverty for the Lakota, who were being systematically displaced and moved to reservations. It was a time when many felt the pain of inequality—of being marginalized and treated as second-class citizens.

In the face of this, Canowicakte routinely demonstrated the Spiritual Principle of equality when he met with others. If a man who Canowicakte knew was poor showed up wearing a torn and threadbare jacket, he would say, "That's a beautiful jacket you're wearing. I've been wanting one just like it. Would you be willing to trade it for mine?" They would swap, and the man would leave a bit warmer and wearing a newer, nicer jacket.

When people came to his home, Canowicakte also made a practice of giving them small gifts. "Thank you for coming to see me; it's an honor," he would say. "Here, take this as an expression of my gratitude for your visit." Most of the time, the gift turned out to be something the visitor needed—washcloths, fresh-picked tomatoes, a piece of cloth, or a few yards of rope.

When Canowicakte died, some people wanted to put a small monument on his grave, but the other elders said no. "Canowicakte wouldn't want anything special," one of them explained. "He'd want us to remember him as one of us, not as someone bigger or better."

Questions for contemplation:

1. Think of a time in your past when you were in a privileged position—when you had special status or connections. Did you feel entitled to this privilege? Did you take advantage of it? How?

2. Think of a current situation in your work or personal life where things are not as equal as you'd like them to be—and where you benefit from this inequality. What practical things can you do to make the situation less unequal in the future?

3. As of right now, where do you place yourself on the continuum from inequality to equality?

Apathy	Care

Apathy

We use apathy to try to avoid hurt. We believe that if we don't care, and if we're not intimately connected to anything or anyone, then nothing and no one can hurt us. We emotionally withdraw from what we believe is a dangerous, cruel, and meaningless world.

Apathy shuts us off from the mystery of the Divine because it kills our questioning and curiosity. We no longer stand on the edge of knowing and ask, "What's next?"

Apathy suppresses our passions, our excitement, and our spiritual craving for things that ask us to celebrate, honor, enjoy, and learn from them.

Apathy is a form of spiritual stagnation. Ultimately, apathy is a refusal to gather our energies and to bind them to positive Spiritual Principles. Apathy is also a refusal to invest ourselves in life. As a result, meaning leaches out of our life, our heart and mind start to shrink, and we become spiritually and intellectually lazy (and often physically lazy as well).

Apathy can also be dangerous. The energy that apathy blocks or holds back can build up and explode, sometimes resulting in abuse or violence toward others—and sometimes in violence toward ourselves.

Care

Care offers us clear, simple, useful direction. So many decisions in life can be handled just by asking ourselves, "Is this a caring thing to do?" and heeding the answer.

Every action and decision needs to pass the care test. If it doesn't, our course is clear and simple: don't do it. Caring thus trumps desire, habit, tradition, and loyalty.

This means that when caring aligns with desire (or habit or tradition or loyalty), we can lean into that desire (or habit or tradition or loyalty) with a clear conscience.

Care is always about relationships: We care for, we care about, we take care of. Care activates our passions and helps us become actively and positively involved in the world. When we care for others and allow others to care for us, we're spared loneliness and isolation.

Care is a softening Principle; it takes the rough edges off our instinctual responses. As my friend Brad, who is a recovering cocaine addict, told me, "Ever since I've learned how to turn my will and life over to the *care* of my Higher Power, I'm not as afraid. My tone is softer with my family and friends. I feel less tense and brittle. I like getting up in the morning again."

Peter's Story

After his older sister died when he was nine years old, Peter stopped playing with his friends and spent more and more time alone. He also started to become a bit of a bully. He was taller than the other kids his age, and he liked the way he could scare them with his mean looks, fast legs, and threats. He rarely actually hit anyone, but he often threatened to. He also sometimes made fun of people and the way they seemed to think that so many things were important. Peter knew better. He had learned

that anyone could die at any time, which to him meant that car-
ing about people got you hurt and was a waste of effort.

    Peter lived in the city, but his mother had grown up on a
farm, and the family would often go to his grandparents' home
in the country. On one of these visits, Peter's grandmother had a
present waiting for him: a baby duck. His grandmother put it in
his hands and said, "It just hatched this morning. If you promise
to be very careful with it, you can have it and raise it." Peter sat
on the ground and stared at this new life in his hands. He had
never felt anything so alive and so soft. "Mom," he said, "I can
feel its heart beating."

    Soon Peter started to change. Every day he would sit with
his duck, feed her, give her water, and play with her. Over the
next few weeks, they developed a game of chasing each other
around the backyard. The duck, which Peter named Ozzie,
became Peter's best friend.

    Peter became friendlier to the other children. How could
he be a bully when his best friend was a duck? Eventually, the
other kids began to come by and ask to pet or hold Ozzie, and
Peter would say, "Okay, as long as you're very careful."

    Peter became a minor celebrity in the neighborhood because
every day he would put a leash on Ozzie and take her for a
walk.

    One day, tragedy struck. Ozzie got out of her pen and was
hit by a car. Peter was brokenhearted. Over the next few weeks,
he started to change back into the old, bullying Peter. Now that
he didn't have his duck to chase, he started chasing the smaller
children once more.

    Then, one day, there was a knock on Peter's front door. He
answered it. There stood five of the kids he had been mean to,
carrying a cardboard box with a baby duck in it. Peter started
to cry.

    He let the kids in and led them onto the back porch, where
they all sat on the floor and played with Peter's new duck.

Questions for contemplation:

1. Is there something in your life that you feel you *should* care about, but don't? Imagine yourself getting involved with this activity, cause, person, or situation. How might adding care change things?

2. Recall a time or event in your life when you acted with great care toward someone. What did it feel like? Did the caring come naturally, or did you have to step past some internal resistance? What were the results of your actions?

3. As of right now, where do you place yourself on the continuum from apathy to care?

Shame	Guilt

Shame

Shame makes us feel bad for the sake of feeling bad, whereas guilt makes us feel bad in order to learn, change, and grow.

Shame tells us that we are inherently unworthy. It has us believe we're unfit to be a full part of humanity—that we are *less than*, and that there is nothing we can do to change this.

Shame is self-reinforcing. It encourages us to behave in ways that trigger or create more shame. Thus when we operate from shame, we become much more vulnerable to betraying ourselves, our values, our relationships, our community, and/or the Divine. The more intense our shame, the more likely we are to seek refuge in other negative spiritual principles. Over time, we can begin to live a lifestyle of shame.

Often, people trapped in their shame then use shame as a tool against others in an attempt to dominate or control them. As a counselor, I often deal with people who have wounds created by shaming teachers, spouses, coaches, clergy, and parents.

Shame-based people often connect with others who reinforce their shame. As my client Abbey explained, "My father told me for years that I was a stupid, no-good loser. Was it any accident that when I got to junior high, the only kids I felt comfortable with were the "losers"—the other kids with low self-esteem? Of course, I got poor grades and acted like a loser, too. It wasn't until I got to college—and I'm not sure how I got there—that things changed for me. I had a professor who believed in me. He confronted me one day and called me a brilliant woman who loved to play stupid. That's when I started changing things around. My grade point average in college went up to 3.8, and I never accepted any of my father's shaming again. Now I can see he was trying to stick me with his own shame and self-hatred."

Blame is a variation of shame. It's a game of musical chairs with the loser getting stuck with the shame. That is why many families and couples will argue about the tiniest of things—because the loser, the one who gives in, must then carry the shame of the family system or the relationship.

Guilt

Guilt is situational. It's not based on what we *are*, but on what we *have done*. It pushes us to make friends with our imperfections and to learn from them, so that we can grow and do the next right thing.

We're all imperfect, all incomplete, all guilty of a variety of mistakes. In fact, part of the great value of guilt is that it tells us when we have made a mistake. Shame, on the other hand, tells us that we *are* a mistake.

The beauty of guilt is in how it activates our conscience. It tells us that we have stepped away from our values or are ignoring a positive Spiritual Principle. This makes our admission of guilt an important and transformative event. It allows a change—a beginning—to occur. (Even the phrase *admission of guilt* speaks of an entry into something new.) Only when we can see, accept, and say that we are wrong can we fix the situation.

A huge part of self-development—whether it takes place

through therapy, life coaching, a Twelve Step group, religious or spiritual practices, or simple self-reflection—is being able to step back, notice what we are guilty of, and admit it. This is a normal part of any healthy relationship.

Leon's Story

When Leon was four years old, his father abandoned him and his mother. His last words to Leon before he left were, "Son, I love you and your mother, but I can't handle it anymore. I've got to go. You be good, now."

Growing up, Leon tried to be good, but he never felt good enough. Deep down he felt that he was to blame for his father leaving the family. This created a great deal of shame for Leon.

When Leon turned twenty-five, he married his girlfriend, Glenda, and two years later their son, Dino, was born. Leon often worried that he would become a bad father, just like his own father had been. This fear grew worse when Glenda died in a boating accident, and a grieving Leon was left to raise his son on his own.

As Dino grew up, Leon gave Dino almost everything he asked for, and he rarely asked Dino to do chores or help out around the house. Leon told himself that he just wanted Dino to be happy, but deep down, Leon was also terrified of being a bad father.

And Dino wasn't happy. When he was nine, he was caught stealing baseball cards from the neighborhood drugstore. Leon paid for the cards and told Dino to be more careful. Dino stole several toys a few weeks later. When Leon discovered them, with their price tags still on, he lectured Dino but didn't punish him.

As Dino grew older, he began stealing bigger and bigger things. In ninth grade, he stole a car and was caught when it ran out of gas on the freeway. Leon picked him up at the juvenile detention center, got a good lawyer for his son, and enabled him to avoid any consequences except for forty hours of volunteer work, which Dino completed grudgingly.

When Dino turned sixteen, he began doing cocaine. Within a few months he became addicted, and on Christmas Day, while high, he drove his car into a creek. Dino escaped with only minor injuries, but for Leon, this was a wakeup call. He insisted that Dino enter a drug treatment program, and Leon began to attend Al-Anon meetings.

Leon began to see how, out of his own shame and his fear of becoming like his own father, he had failed his son in a different way. He had protected Dino too well and made his life too easy.

In Leon's Al-Anon group, he talked about his shame and his fear that he wasn't a good father. Over time, he was able to transform his shame into an honest admission of his strengths, his weaknesses, and his mistakes as a dad. He also began to see ways in which he could become a better father.

Six months after graduating from his treatment program, Dino began doing cocaine again. A few weeks after that, he was caught breaking into someone's home. He called Leon from the detention center and said, "Dad, it sucks here. Come and get me out."

Leon replied, "No, not tonight. Stay overnight and we can talk in the morning. If you still want me to come and get you then, we'll need to have a talk about responsibility and consequences."

"Stay overnight! What kind of a dad are you?"

The words sent a pang through Leon, but he said, "Son, I've done plenty of things wrong as your father, and on those I'm guilty as charged. But I've done some things right, too. And today the right thing to do is to help you begin to learn about consequences. I'm going to my Al-Anon meeting now. Think about what I've said, get some sleep if you can, and we'll talk tomorrow."

Questions for contemplation:

1. Think back to a time when you shamed someone else. What emotions were you feeling that encouraged you to do this? How did the other person respond? How did the situation turn out? If you were to find yourself in a similar situation now, what would you do differently?

2. Think of a time when admitting your guilt to someone else helped you solve or transform a problem. What did you say and do? What did they say and do in response? How did the situation turn out?

3. As of right now, where do you place yourself on the continuum from shame to guilt?

Cowardice

Cowardice is a failure to act wisely and compassionately—or to act at all—because of fear. We all become cowardly from time to time, abandoning Spirit and retreating into instinct, but it does not have to become a way of life.

When we are stuck in cowardice, we listen to and believe the frightened messages coming from our reptilian brain. (We may also repeat them to ourselves over and over.) We then sidestep our responsibility to act according to positive Spiritual Principles. Instead, we seek sanctuary in avoidance, denial, or negative spiritual principles like despair, arrogance, hate, or cynicism. Emotionally, and sometimes literally, we run or we freeze in place.

Often, cowards are angry people. Because cowards are afraid to feel and deal with their own fear, sadness, or sense of powerlessness in constructive ways, they transform these feelings into anger.

There are two ways to get power: by building something or by destroying something. Cowards seek to destroy. In their destructive acts, they unconsciously hope to flee from their own fears, sadness, or powerlessness by implanting it in others.

Cowards tend to hang around together and act in groups. This enables them to feel less frightened and less alone. They may also act in secret or in the dead of night or with their faces covered, so that their cowardice is not exposed. Gangs are classic examples of mass cowardice.

Courage

Courage requires us to go against our instincts, which tell us to attack, defend, freeze, or run. Courage requires us to take a stand and to act with integrity and intention.

Courage is not the same as fearlessness or certainty. In fact, when we act courageously, we often feel doubt or fear. Courage is the ability—and the willingness—to do the next right thing *in spite of* our doubt and fears.

Charlene, a woman I know who had developed a meth addiction, acted with great courage when she showed up at a crisis center with her baby in her arms and asked for help. "I'm an addict," she said, "and my baby deserves better. Will you help me find someone to watch her, and help me get treatment so I can be a good mother?"

We often act with courage in important situations. But courage needs to be a living Principle, one that we practice on a daily basis, in all kinds of situations. We can use courage to confront and challenge ourselves, to see the world in new ways, to be vulnerable, and to change our attitude and mind. All of these forms of courage have something in common: a willingness to step outside our comfort zone and move beyond our own personal status quo.

Some people see themselves as courageous because they're not afraid to challenge or stand up to anyone. Genuine courage, however, isn't about fearlessness. It's about acting wisely and compassionately in all situations. It's about fearlessly standing up to yourself and demanding yourself to do what you know is right and moral.

We need courage on a daily basis to be the best partner,

the best child, the best friend, the best sibling, the best worker, and the best human being we can be.

Mary and Jim's Story

Mary and Jim never organized a demonstration or started a movement or challenged authority in a highly visible way. They weren't interested in hang gliding or motorcycle racing or parachute jumping. But they were a deeply courageous couple nevertheless.

When they learned that they couldn't have children, they spent a year searching their souls and talking about what they should do. Eventually, they decided that they would adopt.

A social worker they knew introduced Jim and Mary to four siblings—two brothers and two sisters, ages two through nine—who had just been put up for adoption. They had been raised by a single mother who was an alcoholic and who had recently become seriously depressed. The three youngest children suffered from fetal alcohol syndrome, and all four had been diagnosed with learning disabilities.

Mary and Jim were not naïve. They understood that these children would have serious problems—and could cause problems for others—for the rest of their lives, no matter how much love and caring they received. Nevertheless, after talking it over, they made the decision to raise those four kids.

For the next nineteen years, their primary focus became raising these children. This was a twenty-four-hour-a-day job. Because the kids took so much of their time, energy, attention, and money, Jim and Mary lost several friends and spent much less time with their extended families. As parents, they suffered much heartache but also experienced great joy. Each day they acted with renewed commitment, knowing that they would face new challenges and unpleasant surprises.

People who knew Mary and Jim often talked about their everyday courage and their willingness to do the next right thing in the face of their worries and fears. One of their friends described Jim and Mary as "angels who gave up their wings in order to care for those kids."

Questions for contemplation:

1. Think of an incident in which you felt an urge to act out of cowardice but acted from courage instead. What were the results? Why did you choose to act from courage? Are you glad you chose courage? Why?

2. All of us have acted out of cowardice at times, and all of us are tempted to act cowardly on a regular basis. When you feel the impulse to act cowardly, what form does this impulse take? What rationale goes through your mind? What emotions do you feel?

3. As of right now, where do you place yourself on the continuum from cowardice to courage?

Unmanaged Fear	Faith

Unmanaged Fear

To be human is to have fear. It's a natural part of our instinctual side. But because we also have minds and reason, we have choices. We don't just see the path that instinct would have us take; often, we see many paths. *Have I chosen correctly? Am I doing the right things? Could I do more?* Our fears can keep us from asking these questions and blind us to many potential paths. If fear and instinct are not properly managed, they can create more harm than protection.

Fear creates a need for a response, a choice point where we either respond with avoidance or control—the options of instinct—or turn to positive Spiritual Principles.

Fear is an internal reaction to a sense of danger, either real or imagined. Its function is to provide us with the energy to either flee or fight. This can save our life in genuinely dangerous situations. But we also often react with fear when there is no genuine danger—when someone criticizes us, or corrects us, or makes fun of us, or cuts us off in traffic. These fears need to be managed. We need to channel them from our reptilian brain to our neocortex for conscious, careful processing. This is important, because unmanaged fear can trap us in an inappropriate fight, flee, or freeze response.

Faith

Faith means placing confidence and trust in something outside of ourselves—or something spiritual within. It is an act of spiritual expansion, a sense that our life will have meaning and purpose if we allow it to be guided by positive Spiritual Principles.

Faith is found not in attitudes, preaching, or slogans, but in actions. Living with faith, we understand that we are not always able to have guarantees before we act. Faith has us walk into problems mindfully, rather than avoid them or try to punch our way through them. Faith is thus the antidote to fear.

Because of faith, we can respond to the many unknowns of life with compassion and wisdom instead of with anger, aggression, or avoidance.

Sometimes faith is a gift bestowed upon us, such as when others have faith in us. At other times, faith grows within as we practice positive Spiritual Principles.

Faith is gentle but strong. It heals, transforms, and comforts us. It speaks to us of the positive future each of us can have if we practice positive Spiritual Principles in all our affairs and do the next right thing. It helps us dig deeper, looking for new spiritual treasures. It helps us believe in transformation and change because it regularly creates transformation and change. Most of all, however, faith pushes us to embrace our purpose.

Marian's Story

Joyce and Don moved into a new neighborhood and immediately became friends with their neighbor to the north. But Marian, their neighbor to the south, ignored Joyce when she walked by and waved. Twice, when Joyce tried to talk to her, Marian answered her curtly and then walked away.

Then, one day, the police came to Joyce's door. They told her there'd been a complaint from next door: The crying of Joyce's newborn baby, who had colic, had kept Marian awake at night.

Joyce was determined to make the situation better. So she baked one of her blackberry pies, which had won an award at the state fair, and put it in her open south window to cool. A few minutes later, she picked up her baby in one arm and the pie in the other, walked to Marian's front door, and rang the doorbell. Before Marian could answer, she leaned down and put her head against Marian's open window. "Hey, neighbor!" she shouted. "I brought you a fresh blackberry pie to eat and the cutest baby on the block to tickle. And if there's something you're mad at me about, come on out and tell me what it is, so I can make it right."

Marian opened the front door and poked her head out. "You know perfectly well why I'm unhappy. I'm surprised others haven't complained."

Joyce handed her the pie. "For you, honey. Talk to me now, so I can be a better neighbor."

"All that noise you people make. The late-night singing, the motorcycle your husband rides, the crying baby . . ."

"Yeah, Don's in a barbershop quartet, and they practice here some nights. I'm sorry. I can have them knock off by ten o'clock, and I can close the south-facing windows. Have you ever been on a motorcycle?"

"No, and I—"

"We've got an extra helmet. I'll have Don give you a ride as soon as he gets home. Eat a piece of pie, and he should be over in a few minutes." She took her infant's arm and waved it at Marian. "Say bye-bye."

After Joyce left, Marian took a bite of the pie. It was so good that she ate two pieces.

When Don pulled up in her driveway a few minutes later, Marian came out to shoo him away—but before she could, he said, "Hi! Ever ridden a horse?"

"Yes, when I was young."

"It's like a horse, only more fun—and, the way I ride, a lot safer. I'll take you for a slow spin around the park."

As she climbed on the motorcycle behind Don, Marian asked, "How do I know I can have faith in your driving?"

"Ask my congregants," Don said as they pulled into the street. "I'm the minister at Aldrich Methodist Church."

Questions for contemplation:

1. Think of an incident in your life in which you allowed fear to control your actions. What exactly were you afraid would happen? What did you do in reaction to those fears? Did those reactions bring harm to anyone, including you? Did what you were afraid of come to pass?

2. Life is uncertain and unpredictable, yet faith enables us to move forward in the face of the unknown. Is there something in your life right now that scares you, yet your faith tells you that you must do something about it soon? Can you take that leap of faith? What action can you take to begin moving forward?

3. As of right now, where do you place yourself on the continuum from unmanaged fear to faith?

| Entitlement | Selflessness |

Entitlement

Entitlement is dangerous because it is a lie. We are not entitled to anything. We have been given much: life, choices, a mind, a heart, and a spirit. Beyond these, however, nothing is guaranteed—and even these will be taken away eventually when we die.

We often take refuge in entitlement when we want to avoid something—usually a painful responsibility, activity, or decision. We tell ourselves that we get to play by special rules or live by different standards than others. Think of the Wall Street money manager who believes he is entitled to a half-million dollar bonus, even though his company lost billions, or the father who demands respect from his children, even though he beats and demeans them.

Entitlement pulls us into the self and inflates our ego. If practiced on a regular basis, it breeds laziness, arrogance, resentment, and other negative spiritual principles. It tells us that our needs, wants, and desires are legitimate but other people's aren't, and that others should cater to us. It pits people against each other. Perhaps most dangerous of all, it separates rights from responsibilities. (In real life, of course, the two naturally go together.)

I remember counseling a family in which the son, a

twenty-seven-year-old man, demanded that his parents allow him to move back into their home. He insisted, "I didn't ask to be born! You had me, so you're responsible for me! I'm entitled by birth to live with you." He was terrified of having to go out into the world and put together a life. By retreating into entitlement, he was able to pretend to himself that he didn't have to shoulder the same responsibilities as every other adult.

Selflessness

We practice selflessness when we allow ourselves to recognize a greater purpose or greater good, and then direct our energies and actions toward that greater good. We put our own personal ambitions and desires aside, and align the well-being of our Spirit with the well-being of others' Spirits.

Paradoxically, because selflessness counters self-absorption by promoting self-sacrifice for a greater good, it increases self-esteem. It also increases intimacy, wisdom, and love.

Through selflessness we care for and love others as ourselves and break down the borders we place between ourselves and others.

Mitchell's Story

As a child, Mitchell had a temper and knew how to use it. He once bit another child because the boy didn't stop calling him "Mr. Mitchell."

Sometimes, when Mitchell's temper got the best of him, his mom would calmly send him to his room with instructions to "stay there until you can act like a decent human being." Mitchell's mom often used the phrase decent human being *when she was talking about expecting people to meet the basic moral standards that everyone should follow to get along with each other.*

His aunt and uncle visited Mitchell and his parents often. They really cared about Mitchell and sometimes took care of him when his parents weren't available. Once his aunt and uncle were leaving to drive back to their home and stopped in Mitchell's room to say good-bye; he had been sent there yet again to stay until he could act like a "decent human being." He was lying facedown on his bed, tears running down his cheeks. His aunt asked him if he was ready to leave his room yet. Mitchell replied, "No. You know, sometimes it's just so hard to act like a decent human being." His aunt smiled, and after hugs and kisses were given, she let Mitchell continue to lie on his bed and think about what it meant to act like a "decent human being."

Through much parental and sibling love, extra guidance and training in impulse control from his parents, and participation in sports, where he learned discipline and cooperation skills, Mitchell's energies became tied more to selflessness and the greater good of his family and his teams than his own sense of entitlement.

When Mitchell was twelve, his uncle asked him what he wanted for Christmas, and he responded, "Uncle, I have everything I need. Would you be willing to take the money you would have used to buy me a Christmas present and donate it to a local charity—maybe the food shelf?"

Maybe more of us need to go to our rooms, lie on our beds, and not come out until we can act like a "decent human being" like Mitchell.

Questions for contemplation:

1. Is there anything you feel that you're entitled to that others are not because of your age, abilities, education, experience, nationality, race, gender, religious background, or personal history? Which other people do you feel aren't entitled to it? Why?

2. Think of a recent incident in which you put your own desires aside and acted selflessly. What happened as a result of your selfless action? In retrospect, are you glad you did what you did?

3. As of today, where do you place yourself on the continuum from entitlement to selflessness?

Deceit   **Integrity**

Deceit

Through deceit, we conceal, misrepresent, or distort truth in order to get what we want. Often, this is power, control, or the upper hand in a relationship. Often, it is control of information.

Tom and Estelle lost their home in eleven months of day-trading stocks. But they never mentioned this to their kids, who were away at college, because they were ashamed of the poor financial decisions they had made. They simply told the kids, "We decided to move to someplace smaller and closer to downtown."

Beth, an oxycodone addict, had five different prescriptions from five different doctors, which she filled at five different pharmacies. This deceit enabled her to hide her addiction from others.

Therese took a sick day, allowing her to be home when her credit card bill came. She knew it would show charges from her out-of-control shopping. Her husband asked her where the bill had gone, and Therese said, "I haven't seen it since the day I paid it. I wonder if I misfiled it somewhere."

Common to all deceit is a desire to avoid the consequences of decisions we made and actions we took. Behind deceit is a fear that if the truth were known, we (or other people we care about) would be harmed. Often, this fear is valid.

We often think of deceit in terms of misleading others, but

in fact, self-deceit is the most common form of deceit. Our instinctual side misleads us often. It has us believe in fears that have little or no basis in reality. It tells us that we can do things that we can't, or have abilities that we don't. It tells us there will not be consequences for actions, even though our neocortex knows there will be.

Integrity

Integrity helps us define who we are, what we stand for, and what we believe in. We practice integrity when we harmonize our everyday life with our value system, and when we match our actions to our words. Integrity thus creates an inner wholeness that we and others around us can come to rely on.

When we operate from integrity, we seek not to gain power but to represent ourselves honestly and truthfully. Integrity involves a trust and faith that principled actions solve problems.

As with many other positive Spiritual Principles, a large part of integrity is about saying no and setting boundaries. When we say no to certain people, situations, and activities that compromise our values, we direct energy away from them and make it available to support our values and positive Spiritual Principles.

Val's Story

Val was a smart woman who played many different roles as a back-office employee for a local chain of restaurants. One of her duties was doing the bookkeeping for the company.

After Val had been at the company for two years, her boss retired and she got a new one. Val and Kat got along very well, and Kat gave Val lots of praise — much more then Val's previous boss had.

At the end of February, while doing the company books, Val noticed some expenses that didn't look quite right. She brought *them to Kat, who promised to look into them and get back to her. About a week later, Kat stuck her head in Val's office. "I checked out those expenses you showed me. They're legit." Still, something didn't seem quite right to Val. But she let it go.*

About three months later, Val found some more irregularities — but this time they were larger. She immediately brought them to Kat. Kat looked at them and nodded silently. Immediately, Val realized that Kat was taking money from the company — and that Kat knew that Val now knew about her.

Kat said quietly, "Val, I got myself in some temporary financial problems and borrowed a little from the company. I'll be paying the money back shortly. Would you please look the other way on this for another couple of weeks?"

Val got up, saying nothing, and walked out of the room. What do I do? *she wondered.* I like her, but this is wrong.

Val didn't sleep at all that night. But in the morning she knew what to do.

As soon as she got to work, she walked into the president's office. With tears in her eyes, she said, "I found out something about Kat that you need to know."

Questions for contemplation:

1. Think about the last time you deceived someone. Why did you feel this deceit was necessary? What emotions were you feeling at the time? What were the results of your deceit? How might you make amends for that deceit now?

2. Think of someone who you believe has a great deal of integrity. What specific things have they said and done that impressed you? What, if anything, prevents you from following that person's lead and acting the way they do?

3. As of right now, where do you place yourself on the continuum from deceit to integrity?

Unkindness	Grace

Unkindness

Unkindness is a refusal to be sensitive to others' needs—or, sometimes, to our own. It is also a refusal to believe in and be part of humanity's collective conscience. Through unkindness, we often take our own unresolved pain or fear and infect others with it. *Because I hurt, someone must pay.*

We can all have unkind thoughts about others. We may hope that they will suffer or secretly rejoice when things go badly for them. We can also have unkind thoughts about ourselves, blaming and chastising ourselves for honest mistakes and misjudgments.

When unkindness partners with other negative spiritual principles, such as arrogance and cynicism, it can be a source of perverse pleasure for us. Arthur had a wicked sense of humor; he made people laugh, but often his humor was at others' expense. Over time, however, he slowly became aware of his unkindness. He said, "I saw my biting humor as humor; others just saw it as biting."

Grace

Grace occurs in those moments when Spirit trumps instinct.

Grace is an opening up, an expansion, a willingness to give over more of ourselves to a spiritual life. It is often a gift bestowed on us. It is also a gift we can bestow on others—and on ourselves.

Grace increases ethical power. Sometimes it also allows miracles to happen. The converse is also true: The more we live in harmony with positive Spiritual Principles, the more we open ourselves up to grace.

Grace creates a shift from negative to positive thinking and creates options where before there were none. Our internal fighting ceases, and our energies get redistributed in a positive way.

Grace encompasses the whole brain; when we are touched by grace, new perspectives and new insights will naturally appear to us. Doing good works, doing the next right thing, and resisting the siren song of negative spiritual principles—all of these things make sense and feel right.

All things spiritual have grace embedded in them.

Lotta's Story

Lotta grew up in southern Sweden, in a home where she endured years of alcoholism, frequent abandonment, and physical and sexual abuse. The only pleasant times she remembered were visits to her grandparents' farm, where she got to play with the cows and bring them in for milking. Lotta liked the cows because they, unlike humans, didn't want to harm her.

As a teenager, Lotta began living on the streets, where she fell into a lifestyle of danger and misery. She became a heroin addict who survived by selling drugs and stealing. Having only been exposed to unkindness her whole life—and been forced to absorb the hurt, pain, and fear of others—she only knew to extend the same to herself.

Once or twice a year, she would enter a treatment center for her addiction, but she would always leave once the process of surrender and healing became too painful. Each time, she would return to the streets.

Then, one day, during her fifth attempt at treatment, she experienced grace. She was in group therapy, being heavily confronted about some of the bad choices she had been making at the center. She suddenly stood up and shouted, "The hell with all of you! I don't need you! I don't need anyone!"

She stormed out the door and walked down the path toward a farmer's field, crying and screaming at the heavens. "If there's something up there, then, damn it, tell me what to do! Show yourself and tell me what to do!"

When her eyes focused again, she realized she was beside a fence; on the other side was a herd of cows. Lotta, remembering happier days on the farm with her grandparents, moved to pet the cows standing along the fence.

Swedish farmers attach nametags to their cows' ears. The first cow Lotta encountered was named "Stop." The second cow she saw was named "Will." The third cow was named "Live." Three cows: Stop—Will—Live.

Her Higher Power had delivered the message to her through the only creatures on Earth that she trusted: cows.

She went back to the treatment center and told her counselor and group what had happened. Her counselor was smart enough to say little. Instead, she got a camera, took pictures of the cows, and gave them to Lotta. These photos reminded Lotta of the miracles that can sometimes happen when we ask for them and open up to them.

Lotta has been sober now for more than sixteen years. She works with women who have been abused and who live on the streets. She gave me a set of the photos, which I keep on my desk and often use in my talks.

Questions for contemplation:

1. Think of a recent incident in which you were unkind to someone else. What were the results of your unkindness? If you were to find yourself in a similar situation now,

what would you do differently? Now think of a recent time when you were unkind to *yourself*. What were the results of your unkindness? If you were in a similar situation again, would you treat yourself differently? How?

2. Think back to a time when you felt grace at work in your life. Recall the incident or period in detail. What were the immediate results of that grace? What were the long-term results? Can you still see some of the effects of that grace in your life now?

3. As of right now, where do you place yourself on the continuum from unkindness to grace?

Impatience	Patience

Impatience

Impatience is an immature relationship with time, an unwillingness to accept difficulty and uncertainty in the here and now, and a refusal to wait for results that can only manifest through the passage of time.

As mortal beings, we each have a limited amount of time. Time thus defines and confines us. But positive Spiritual Principles are not trapped in time; they are ongoing, timeless, eternal, stable. This is one of the reasons we need to surrender to them—for the gift of stability they can give us in the midst of our impatience and limitations.

When something undesirable happens, we can easily become impatient. We complain. We become annoyed, restless, or irritable. We speed up. We try to quickly fix the situation. All these are attempts to control something we can't control: time. The one thing we don't do is stay in the moment.

A friend who had been quite impatient in his earlier life spent ten years disciplining himself with daily rituals of meditation and yoga. He told me, "The biggest gift I've received from my training is a deeper, richer relationship with my values, and with the present moment. I now know how to stop, look past the chatter in my mind at what's before me, and reflect on what fits with my spiritual beliefs. I'm so much less reactive and impatient. Before, I lived life like a squirrel on amphetamines."

Patience

Patience is the ability to stay in our neocortex—the reasoning part of our brain—and to practice positive Spiritual Principles, even when the pains of life make us want to go reptilian and become defensive and reactive. Through patience, we can stay composed and caring during difficult times and in challenging situations. Patience allows us to alter our relationship with time.

Patience enables us to stay in the moment, which is the only place and time where we can access ethical power. In the moment, we can decide (or discover) which positive Spiritual Principle will best guide us right now. We can then surrender our energies to that Principle, allowing us to *respond* from our spiritual side rather than *react* from our reptilian brain.

Fear, pain, and other forms of suffering create in all of us a natural desire for relief, comfort, and the indulging of passions. In the midst of this suffering, patience allows these desires to be transformed into spiritual growth. Patience enables us to continue to place principles before ego, values before desires, and care before self-interest. We can then do the next right thing rather than chase after our own imagined source of comfort or relief.

Some practices that help us stay present and patient include yoga, meditation, the martial arts, prayer, deep breathing, and quiet reflection. All of these feed our drive for meaning and help us stay centered in our neocortex.

Ted's Story

As the boys and girls in Master Yen's martial arts class practiced their kicks and throws, Master Yen could tell that something wasn't right. The energy was too fast; he could feel his students' impatience and aggressiveness growing. Most were in a hurry to learn and improve. As a result, one of the boys fell improperly and sprained his arm.

At the end of the class, Master Yen told his students that on Saturday he would have something new and wonderful to teach them. Immediately, he felt his students' excitement grow.

Saturday arrived. Master Yen entered the dojo and announced, "Today, you learn to sit." The twelve boys and girls looked at each other as if he were crazy.

Master Yen told his students to sit comfortably on the floor. He sat down with them. "Now," he said, "we'll all sit in silence for an hour."

Ted was one of the younger boys. His head quickly filled with thoughts. Why is he doing this? Is he punishing us? What are we supposed to learn from this? What a waste of time! My legs are starting to hurt. Maybe I should quit and go home. Boy, does Nancy look angry. *And so on and so on.*

After an hour, Master Yen announced that there would be a five-minute break, during which he expected everyone to remain silent.

At the end of the break, Master Yen told everyone that they would sit silently for another hour. Ted felt a rush of anger as he sat down, but he took a few deep breaths and settled back into a comfortable position.

The second hour was different. After a time, his mind stopped racing. Ted focused on his breathing, allowing it to simply flow in and out.

His thinking stopped, and the floor seemed to open up before him. He saw a field and could hear birds. He felt himself drifting through the air, up and down the hills and valleys. He could feel the wind against his face.

He didn't know how long this continued. But suddenly he felt a tap on his shoulder.

He was back in the dojo, sitting on the floor, with Master Yen standing next to him. Master Yen said to the class, "Three of you received the gift of patience today. The rest of you did not. Class is over for today."

Most of the class felt frustrated—but three children, including Ted, slowly stood up and bowed to Master Yen.

A year later, nine of the children had quit the class. Ted and two others—those who had experienced patience—continued, and were joined by ten new students. The three who had shown patience had become role models for the others, and their kicks and throws were the most accurate, precise, and well timed.

Questions for contemplation:

1. In what situations are you most likely to become impatient? What person or people do you most often become impatient with? What do you think would happen if, the next time you felt impatient, you let yourself *feel* impatient but *acted* with patience?

2. Who are you most patient with? Why? What would happen if you were equally patient with everyone? If you were just as patient with yourself?

3. As of right now, where do you place yourself on the continuum from impatience to patience?

Self-Righteousness	Anonymity

Self-Righteousness

In being self-righteous, we place ourselves above others in an attempt to create dominance, distance, or both. We see ourselves as having clearer perception than other people. And we are not only quite sure that we are right; either outwardly or secretly, we also want others to recognize our rightness. Yet underneath our self-righteousness is a fear of having our own defects pointed out.

Self-righteousness combines the illusion of moral or intellectual superiority with a refusal to examine our own ideas, beliefs, and character. At the same time, however, we are quite willing to examine—and point out—the flaws in other people's ideas, beliefs, and characters.

Self-righteousness hardens our heart and drains it of empathy. It makes us brittle and cold, and it takes away one of our most valuable spiritual qualities: vulnerability. We can wind up feeling wiser than, better than, or more capable than others—but all alone.

For someone stuck in self-righteousness to become spirituality authentic, they must become vulnerable and step off the pedestal they have placed themselves on. They must use the positive Spiritual Principle of courage to disobey the cardinal rule of self-righteousness: never admit you're wrong.

Anonymity

Spiritual anonymity is not about hiding in the woods. It is about willingly putting positive Spiritual Principles before our own desires — including our desire for personal acknowledgment.

Spiritual anonymity seeks no glory, just the opportunity to do more good deeds and receive the lessons of positive Spiritual Principles. Spiritual anonymity thus counters ego and self-righteousness.

In being anonymous, we learn that personal sacrifice increases self-esteem, dignity, and integrity. If we practice spiritual anonymity regularly, doors open to greater humility, for we see how weak we are compared to positive Spiritual Principles. We also see that our true significance comes from putting positive Spiritual Principles in the full light of the sun, while keeping our ego in the shadows.

In this way, we each offer up a single voice to become part of a choir of many. To our reptilian brains, this may feel like a sacrifice — but, in fact, it's the sharing of something much bigger than any of us.

In the original Olympics in ancient Greece, no records were kept, and no statues were erected to honor the winners. The only people who were considered notable were the eight people who were caught cheating over the years. Statues of these people were erected, and competing athletes walked between these statues in order to enter the Olympic grounds. There was no first, second, or third place. There was glory to the winner, honor to all who participated honestly, and well-publicized guilt for those who cheated to get recognition.

Xenia's Story

Xenia was smart and knew it. Throughout high school, she got As and Bs in all her classes, and she was very popular. A troop of four or five girls followed her around, and many of the boys wanted her to go out with them. Xenia had a sharp tongue that sometimes got her in trouble with teachers, but it always enabled her to win arguments with the other students. She wasn't quite pretty enough or popular enough to be the homecoming queen, but in her clique, she was the queen bee.

When she went to college on a scholarship, she didn't make many friends and soon became something of a loner. She thought that most of her fellow students were uninteresting, weak, and somewhat pathetic.

In her sophomore year, however, she found a home in a church where the minister and the members knew The Truth. The minister preached that anyone not of the faith would go to hell, and Xenia believed him. She worked hard to convert her relatives and her old friends from high school, but everyone was turned off by her self-righteous attitude. By her senior year of college, the only people who would have anything to do with her were her parents and other members of the church.

Xenia fell in love with a man from this church, and they married a year after she graduated. They bought a home and had three children.

Xenia's spiritual crisis came when her third child was born. Simon had only one hand—the other arm ended in a simple lump of flesh—and her minister quickly declared the child to be the work of the devil. He confronted Xenia, asking her what sins she had committed to cause a devil child to develop inside of her. But from the moment Xenia first saw Simon and looked into his eyes, she saw nothing but love. Her hardened heart had melted.

One Sunday, Xenia and her family attended the church service as usual. As Xenia sat there holding Simon, the minister pointed to her and started talking about the devil child and the wages of sin. Xenia stood up, looked him in the eyes, and said, "You pompous old goat, nobody gets to say those things about my beautiful Simon." She looked at her husband and said, "Come on, we're leaving." Their entire family got up and walked out.

Over time, Xenia and her family found a new church home, one where everyone was treated exactly the same. Nobody thought they were special or singled out by God or automatically destined for heaven. No one thought everyone else was destined for hell, either. And as Simon grew older, everyone treated him like the ordinary human child he was.

Today, Xenia speaks with gratitude about how Simon helped save her soul and the soul of the family. His "flaw" brought them all down to earth, took them off their self-righteous pedestals, and helped them see the beauty and goodness in their fellow human beings. "If he had been born with two normal hands, we would have all probably stayed in that first church and drunk the Kool-Aid."

Questions for contemplation:

1. In what situations are you most likely to become self-righteous? With what issues? With what people? Is there a common theme? When you become self-righteous, what effect does that have on others? Is this the effect you want to have on them?

2. Have you ever done good deeds for others anonymously? Can you remember why you wanted to stay anonymous? What effects did your actions have on others? On you? Would the effects have been different if you hadn't been anonymous?

3. As of right now, where do you place yourself on the continuum from self-righteousness to anonymity?

Disdain	Empathy

Disdain

Disdain is more than just a lack of respect; it is contempt for the imperfections (or, in extreme cases, the very existence) of others. Most of all, disdain dismisses others as being unimportant. Disdain does not merely say, "You are shameful"; it says, "You don't deserve to be considered, or to be cared about, or to exist."

Disdain hardens our heart and ossifies our thoughts. Worst of all, it dehumanizes everyone it touches—both the objects of disdain and the people who practice it.

When we're operating from disdain, we don't notice our attitude of superiority. We are too focused on the unworthiness and the inferiority of the other. But what we are really doing is covering up our own insecurities with scorn toward others.

Empathy

Empathy has us partner with the conditions and emotions of others. When we empathize with others, we put aside our own frame of reference in favor of connection, understanding, vulnerability—and, often, shared suffering. Empathy blurs the boundaries between self and others, and shows us that we are all more similar than different.

The ability to feel empathy comes from our neocortex, as empathy involves understanding and visualizing the world-view or emotions of another person. It expands our capacity to carry the suffering of others—and thus it increases our capacity to hold and transform our own suffering as well.

Empathy directs us to reach out to others and share their pain in order to understand, accept, and transform our own pain. It tears down the barriers we place between ourselves and others, helping to create a *we* between two or more *me's*.

Empathy also spreads positive emotions. When we empathize with others who are feeling joy, then we experience joy as well—both for them and with them.

Empathy both precedes and encourages action in service to others. When practiced in groups, empathy also supports the development of community and of collective conscience.

Empathy is not pity, for pity preserves a one-up/one-down hierarchy. Empathy comes from a place where all people are seen as equal.

Paradoxically, when we empathize with someone else, we get a better understanding of ourselves as well, and we open up to having more compassion about our own suffering.

Astrid's Story

Astrid told me about the moment she discovered her life's work. "It was twenty years ago," she explained. "I was twelve years old and very, very spoiled. I would cry and pout whenever I didn't get whatever I wanted. Everything was all about me—I looked down on other people and couldn't care less about their problems. They simply didn't exist to me.

"Then one night my brother was watching a television program about children being sold into slavery. I sat down and watched it with him, and soon saw a girl about my age. In her

eyes I could see that her spirit had been destroyed. Her parents had sold her, and she had been turned into a sex slave.

"I couldn't take my eyes off her eyes. In them I could see all her suffering—the suffering of being abandoned by her parents, and the suffering caused by the hundreds of men who had crawled upon her body, assaulting her innocence. Those sunken, haunted eyes called out for the peace of death.

"It was at that moment I decided I wanted to become a policewoman, and later to be a vice cop. I felt that if I could save just one girl, then maybe I could help make the suffering that girl had gone through mean something.

"To this day, I can close my eyes and see her eyes. Sometimes I have nightmares and hear her crying out to me for help. I've helped hundreds of girls in my career, but I still wonder what happened to that young girl who changed my life—and I still cry for her."

Questions for contemplation:

1. When did you last feel or express disdain? What were the circumstances? What effects did this disdain have on you? On the other person?

2. Is there a person, a cause, or a form of suffering that you have great empathy for? Why? When you're operating from empathy, what other emotions do you feel? Does your thinking change in any way?

3. As of right now, where do you place yourself on the continuum from disdain to empathy?

Skepticism   **Trust**

Skepticism

We often need to seek more or better information in order to question absolutes, prevailing views, and the status quo. Doing so demonstrates curiosity, discernment, and a concern for truth.

The negative spiritual principle of skepticism, however, is something else entirely. It is an iron gate used to lock out new information, new perspectives, and the challenge of growth demanded by spirituality. It is the prejudgment that something can't be true, valid, or valuable. It replaces investigation with dismissal, exploration with inaction, and vulnerability with protectiveness.

Skeptics protect themselves with a barrier of negativity and doubt, through which they attempt to avoid all risk and vulnerability. In the process, however, they also avoid hope, commitment, and much of life's joy.

Skepticism is often the scar tissue overlying an emotional or spiritual wound. Long ago, we took a risk and let ourselves be vulnerable—and, as a result, we got hurt. Not wanting to repeat the experience, we tell ourselves that a less painful, more positive outcome isn't possible. Although this may protect us from further wounding, we also close ourselves off to positive surprises—and to important spiritual lessons.

Trust

Trust is based not in ideas but in action. It is a deliberate turning to a source of guidance, especially when we are in need or afraid.

All of us experience times when our trust in individual people, or in humanity as a whole, is broken. Yet even then we have choices. We can trust positive Spiritual Principles and the Divine—and we can also trust ourselves. Or we can put our faith in negative spiritual principles, or in status, power, money, and other material things. In each new situation and encounter, we get to make this choice anew.

Eventually, all of us learn that there are times to trust people and times not to trust people. We also learn that we, too, are trustworthy at times and untrustworthy at other times.

However, we can work day by day to become more and more trustworthy. We can decide what we stand for and what kind of person we are—and, in each new moment, we can work to do the next right thing.

Helen's Story

Helen was a woman I met through a friend. She agreed to have lunch with me and to let me interview her about her days in Auschwitz, where she survived the experiments she suffered at the hands of Josef Mengele. Helen had every scrap of innocence taken from her in the days before World War II and during her time in captivity. She had every right to become hardened, skeptical, and protective of herself and her vulnerability.

Yet Helen possessed a gentleness, a calmness, and a solid strength. I had expected her to be bitter and untrusting, yet Helen was neither.

Halfway through lunch, I asked her if she felt angry and distrustful of the world. She answered, "Why? Of course I feel sad

*for the family and friends I lost and for the suffering that oc-
curred, but anger and distrust? No, that was their way. I honor
the people who died by teaching others about what happened
and how to live a full and useful life.*

*"I still trust in humanity—not all of it, but most of it. I
made it through the camps by learning to tell who was trustable
and who wasn't. We helped each other survive. There were even
a few guards who were more trustable than others. They would
sneak you extra bread or potatoes if they could.*

*"People come through for you or they don't. You can trust
certain ones but not certain others. That's just the way life is."*

Questions for contemplation:

1. What are three things that you are automatically
   skeptical of? For each of these things, what would it
   take for you to change your skepticism to trust? In
   any of these cases, could your skepticism actually be
   closed-mindedness?

2. Think of three examples of knowledge or wisdom you
   received in exchange for some of your innocence. Have
   you become more trustable or less trustable because of
   these exchanges?

3. As of right now, where do you place yourself on the
   continuum from skepticism to trust?

Infidelity	Commitment

Infidelity

Infidelity isn't just about cheating on our spouse or partner. It's about violating our values or turning away from positive Spiritual Principles.

We commit spiritual infidelity whenever we go against these Principles in an attempt to avoid responsibility, consequences, or pain, or to fulfill our personal desires at another's expense.

Infidelity doesn't occur accidentally; it's a choice, an act of free will. There is usually a moment of guilt that takes place just before we choose infidelity. As one client told me, "I hated that small voice that told me stealing was wrong. It got in the way of the excitement of shoplifting. With practice I was able to get past it—until the day I was arrested."

Infidelity often involves betraying others, but it *always* involves betraying ourselves. We give ourselves away to something we already know to be hurtful or wrong.

A great deal of spiritual infidelity takes place in private: ignoring a letter from a friend who asked for help, looking at porn while our partner is asleep, or fudging on our expense reports. Because these moments of infidelity are private, they can more easily become habitual. Left unchecked over time, however, they can slowly turn into a lifestyle of lying and cheating.

Commitment

Spiritual commitment lines up our will with the essence of positive Spiritual Principles. We surrender many of our personal desires—and the cravings of our reptilian brain—in service of something deeper. Commitment is thus both restrictive and freeing at the same time.

We can only practice commitment over time, for commitment is a decision we make, and an action we take, over and over. In a wide range of new situations, we return to our values and the positive Spiritual Principles rather than chase after those shiny objects of desire that would distract us. Over time, these accumulated choices and actions add up to commitment—and this commitment ultimately transforms us. The longer we stay attached to positive Spiritual Principles through our commitment, the deeper and more profound our personal transformation becomes.

Olivia's Story

Olivia was a nun who was active in the peace movement. She had been arrested many times for her activism and was usually released without being charged.

Olivia was not an angry person. She was not naïve enough to believe that blocking a door at the headquarters of a company that made cluster bombs would change the minds of many of the people inside. She just hoped to create moments in which people would stop to think. She told people, "I'm just a message that needs to be delivered."

After her twenty-ninth arrest, the judge told Olivia that next time she would be sentenced to six months in jail. Four months later, she participated in another protest. She was arrested yet again, and this time, she did get sentenced to six months in jail.

It was here that Olivia met Frank, one of the guards in her detainment area. Frank actually agreed with Olivia on many of her ideas about nonviolent protests, but his allegiance was more to the law than to his own principles.

Frank seemed upset one day, so Olivia asked him what was wrong. He told her that his wife's kidneys were failing and she needed a transplant. Olivia offered to see if her own kidney would be a match. It turned out that Olivia's kidney would work, and within three months, Frank's wife, Kayla, had Olivia's kidney.

A deep friendship developed among the three of them. After long talks about cluster bombs and the damage they do, mainly to civilian women and children, Frank and his family ended up semi-regulars at the local protests, although he chose not to do anything that would get him arrested, because it might cost him his job.

What changed Frank wasn't Olivia's gift of a kidney. This just got his attention. "It was her commitment to a lifestyle of peace, and her commitment to doing what she believed to be right, that caused us to want to get close to her and what she stood for," he says. It's also what nudged him to turn inward, examine his own values, and seek to live them more fully—whether on the job or off. "Today," he reports, "Olivia is my spiritual adviser."

Questions for contemplation:

1. Think about a time in your life when you chose to go against your own values—or against one or more of the positive Spiritual Principles. What emotion prompted you to make that decision? Fear? Anger? Powerlessness? Lust? What were the results of that decision?

2. What three things are you most committed to in your life? Do you consistently act according to those commitments? If not, what specific things can you do to more fully live in and express those commitments?

3. As of right now, where do you place yourself on the continuum from infidelity to commitment?

| Dishonor | Dignity |

Dishonor

We practice dishonor when we go against our own values and beliefs, whether they are stated or unstated. We also act dishonorably when we violate the code of our profession, ignore an agreement we made with others, or fail to carry out a responsibility we have accepted.

Some examples include the following:

- You're a high school teacher. You're supposed to stand for the education, care, and protection of kids. Instead, you take advantage of their innocence and seduce a student.

- You're an investment adviser. You push your clients toward riskier investments than they request because you earn high commissions on them.

- You're a parent and your marriage is in trouble. You actively work to turn your children against your spouse, just to make yourself feel better.

- You're a grandparent. You offer to watch your grandchildren so their parents can have a night off. After supper, however, you get drunk and pass out, leaving the children unsupervised.

People who routinely act dishonorably often work hard to project an image of honor and integrity, while in private they let their reptilian brains take over. These folks aren't interested in conscience, only in a public illusion of conscience. When their misconduct is discovered, people often say things such as, "He seemed like such a good man."

Dignity

Dignity is consistently acting according to our own highest values—and according to positive Spiritual Principles—whether others are watching us or not. Over and over, we do the next right thing, honoring our commitments, serving others, and putting positive Spiritual Principles ahead of our own desires.

If we show up at the park cleanup gathering as we said we would, even though it's rainy and cold, we acquire dignity. If we stop to help a stranded motorist, we acquire dignity. If, while on a business trip, an attractive person flirts with us and invites us to his or her room, we touch our wedding ring and say, "No, I think I'll go to my room and call my spouse," we acquire dignity.

My client Nathan spoke of dignity in terms of his meth addiction and recovery: "For years during my addiction, I had no dignity. I was an animal doing what animals do. I lived in the shadows, stole, lied, lived a life of shame. In recovery, I discovered purpose, and with each act of service, I gained a bit of dignity and walked more upright."

Albert's Story

If you had met Albert a few years ago, you would have thought he was a very nice guy—the type of man you'd want to invite over for dinner. He attended all of his child's functions, appeared to be a good father, and did volunteer work at the local animal shelter.

But out of the public eye, Albert became a different man. He was obsessed with women dressing and undressing. He enjoyed porn, but he enjoyed catching nude and half-clad women with his own video camera far more. After dark, Albert would often make an excuse to leave the house and prowl the streets with his camera, looking for lighted windows in people's bedrooms.

One summer night, a woman's husband caught him crouched behind a bush, pointing his video camera at a slightly open window. The man called the police and let his German shepherd loose. The neighbor and the dog kept Albert cornered until the police arrived.

In searching his apartment, the police found all the videos Albert had made in his voyeur activities. His neighbors and work colleagues were shocked, and many couldn't believe it.

Albert ended up in prison and became a registered sex offender. He took part in a long-term therapeutic community for sex offenders and was eventually paroled. It was difficult for him to go back into his community, but he decided that he would face up to what he had done and try to regain his honor.

Gradually, through doing volunteer work again and making amends to his family, he began to restore his dignity. After some time, he was able to return to the therapeutic community as a mentor to the other sex offenders and gained the respect of his counselors and even the local police. While his family couldn't completely forgive him for the damage he'd done to them, after several years his children started talking to him again and would see him on some holidays and special occasions.

Questions for contemplation:

1. Think of a time in your life when you acted dishonorably—when you made yourself look good, but acted in a way that harmed or exploited someone else. How did you justify this to yourself? To others? What were the results of your dishonorable actions?

2. Think of two choices you've made that have brought you the most dignity. Were they difficult to make? In retrospect, are you glad you made them? In what ways did those choices help or serve others? In what ways did they ultimately benefit you?

3. As of right now, where do you place yourself on the continuum from dishonor to dignity?

Greed		Charity

Greed

Greed is a misinterpretation of the spiritual craving for unity inside of us. It is created by the interplay of our spiritual side and our instinctual side, with our instinctual appetites in control. As my friend Chris says, "Greed is answering the spiritual calling inside of us by going to the wrong address."

Our spirits crave to unite with others and with the eternal, the Divine. This is why we're drawn to positive Spiritual Principles. Greed gets created when we redirect this spiritual craving toward things of a temporal nature, or when we believe that material things can solve our spiritual issues.

Greed pulls us into the most primitive areas of our reptilian brain, where security, safety, and satiation are all that matter. Yet no matter how much greed pursues these, it never produces any of them. Instead, paradoxically, it just produces more greed—and often it increases our fear and dissatisfaction, which can push us toward other negative spiritual principles.

When we are scared, our reptilian brain wants to protect us by acquiring more objects, power, money, or pleasurable experiences. But because fear never actually protects us, we end up greedy, unsatisfied, and just as afraid as before.

Charity

Charity is not a mindset or an idea; it's always a specific act. Charity without action is just wishful intention. But charity is not a transaction, for it seeks nothing in return. It is giving in its purest, most elemental form.

Charity is also a way to honor the blessings and gifts given to us by sharing them with others. Acts of charity often result in humility, for in giving to others we are often humbled by how much has been given to us. In charity we thus often experience fulfillment, a sense that we have (and are) enough. Charity also often brings joy.

Emilio's Story

My new client Emilio explained why he had come to see me:

"I grew up empty. My parents had little time for my sister and me, and we had little time for them and their constant fighting. They spent a lot of their time trying to prove to each other that they were right. To me, it was clear that they were both wrong.

"When I was eight years old, I asked my father for a bicycle. He said, 'Sure, you can have a bike. Go get a job, earn some money, and buy one.' So I got a paper route and earned the money for the bike.

"I still remember that first time I had money of my very own. I felt a great release. I was free of my parents! Instead of being yelled at when I asked them for money, I could earn my own. I was free at last!

"I worked my morning paper route well, and after a short time I also got an evening route. During the winter I shoveled snow, and in the summer I mowed lawns, all of which gave me more money and kept me away from home longer. While my parents fought, I would be in my room going over my savings

accounts and thinking of ways to add to them. As I got older, I read books on money, about men like Rockefeller, and about the stock market.

"I spent very little, for I had a clear goal: to get money and have it work for me earning interest, making more money.

"I paid my way through college working two jobs and rarely saw my parents. I only invited them to graduation to see if they would give me a gift. They gave me a card with ten dollars in it, which I framed and hung on my wall.

"By the time I got out of college, I had started a couple of different businesses and was doing okay in the stock market. I had panic attacks sometimes, though, and the only thing that calmed me was to sit and go over my accounts and remind myself of how much I was worth.

"How did I end up in therapy? I was standing at the meat counter in the supermarket staring at the T-bone steaks. I wanted one very badly, but if I bought it, it meant spending extra money—money I hadn't budgeted for that week. I had only budgeted for hot dogs. Here I was, forty-four years old, never married, working sixty hours a week and driving myself crazy over a steak. I started shaking and tears started running down my cheeks. I was crying uncontrollably—having a major panic attack. I ran out of the store knowing I was in trouble. That's when I decided to pick up the phone and seek help.

"At the time, I was worth over five million dollars."

Over time, Emilio came to see that, despite the wealth he had accumulated and the false sense of security it gave him, he was just as empty as he had felt as a small boy—and just as scared. His therapy involved reaching inside himself to let go of his resentment and insecurities from his childhood. This freed him to become more charitable toward himself and, eventually, others.

Questions for contemplation:

1. Fear often inspires greed. What fears most tempt you to act out of greed? Fear of destitution? Fear of financial insecurity? Fear of losing your partner? Fear of losing your job or career?

2. What is the most charitable thing you've ever done in your life? What effects did this action have on others? On yourself? Have you repeated that act, or done something similar, since then? Why or why not?

3. As of right now, where do you place yourself on the continuum from greed to charity?

Laziness	Perseverance

Laziness

Laziness is not a lack of ability. It is having ability, yet failing or refusing to use that ability to do the next right thing.

Most of us find pleasure in doing nothing at times. Our instinctual side often wants nothing more than a good meal and a nice tree to lie under and nap. There is nothing wrong with fulfilling these desires, up to a point; in fact, sufficient rest and relaxation are important parts of a sane and healthy life.

But laziness is something else entirely. It is an avoidance of life's challenges, a failure to do what needs to be done, a shirking of our responsibilities as an adult human being, and an unwillingness to practice the discipline and dedication needed to put together a moral life.

Practical spirituality and positive Spiritual Principles require regular action. Laziness is a refusal to step into action, to engage with the world, to find and take our place in it. It is only through action that we develop our moral and spiritual power. Laziness allows that power to atrophy.

Laziness does not always involve doing little or nothing, however. There's also a form of laziness in which we focus on relatively unimportant tasks—perhaps we even pour lots of time and energy into them—instead of handling the bigger (and often more immediate) challenges in our lives. We water the plants when we should be repairing the front steps. Or we repair the front steps when we should be having a difficult and painful discussion with our partner about her aging parents, who are no longer physically capable of living in their home without assistance.

Ultimately, laziness is the refusal to accept and respond to the demands and challenges of life.

Perseverance

Perseverance is continued action in pursuit of a goal, even in the face of opposition. In the case of spiritual perseverance, that goal can be deeper and more meaningful connections, the betterment of the world, or a stronger sense of the Divine within and around us.

In persevering, we focus on what is in front of us, on earnest effort, and on pushing past resistance, doubts, fears, and the desire to give up. By persevering, we discover deeper parts of ourselves, and we come to see just what we're capable of, which is often far more than we realized.

Spiritual perseverance also means staying within the boundaries of our value system and the guidelines of positive Spiritual Principles. This includes regularly checking and inventorying our actions and decisions—and, when necessary, correcting ourselves.

Perseverance helps us to stay spiritually on track and to keep our balance under all types of conditions and in the face of multiple temptations. It is the day-to-day reaffirming of the Divine within us through our actions.

Although perseverance begins with our own effort and commitment, often we cannot persevere without the help of others. We may need to reach out and ask for help, support, guidance, and/or inspiration. Perseverance at these times needs to partner with humility, helping us accept our limits and our need for others. And when people persevere as a group, they encourage a strong sense of community.

Lewis's Story

I've known Lewis for more than fifteen years. For many of those years, he was a crack addict. Lewis had been through many rounds of treatment. He would stay sober from his addiction for a time and then relapse. He'd complete more treatment, attend self-help groups, and relapse again; then go to treatment, attend self-help groups, and relapse yet again.

Everyone would put energy and resources into him, and he would work hard for a few months or a year—until ego would trip him up, he'd become lazy in his recovery efforts, and he'd relapse. His illness would pull him back into its ugliness, and he would end up living on people's couches. Over time, most people gave up on Lewis.

But beneath Lewis's many layers of defiance, arrogance, self-centeredness, and entitlement was a genuine desire for recovery and a real love for the people in his recovery community.

Lewis experienced no white lights, no burning bushes. No angels appeared to him, other than the ones who sat next to him in his recovery groups.

Through perseverance and by continually showing up, Lewis finally succeeded. Today he has achieved more than two years of sobriety and enough humility to stay sober. He is now married to a good woman, and they have two beautiful children. He has a business, and he is generous in helping other recovering addicts who some people have given up on.

When someone says, "I don't think I can make it," others say, "Hey, if Lewis can make it, you can make it." He is a wonderful example of the miracle of perseverance.

Questions for contemplation:

1. All of us feel a desire to be lazy at times—but we don't have to follow that desire. Can you think of a time when you followed an impulse to be lazy, but now wish you

hadn't? What do you wish you had done instead? How difficult would that have actually been?

2. Think of a situation where perseverance paid off for you. In what ways did you benefit from your perseverance? In what ways did others benefit? In retrospect, are you glad that you persevered in the face of your or others' doubts and fears?

3. As of right now, where do you place yourself on the continuum from laziness to perseverance?

Resistance

We often resist spiritual growth—or change of any type—even when we know it is best for us. Because we have an instinctual need for security (think of this as our reptilian brain at work), we tend to interpret change as a threat—something to fear and defend against. But when we use our ability to think critically (our neocortex at work), we know better. When change supports connection, growth, or positive Spiritual Principles, our neocortex has the power to overrule our reptilian brain and move forward in spite of our fears and resistance.

As we've seen, any system works to preserve itself by staying in balance. If some force or tension in one part of the system increases or decreases, then other parts of the system shift to maintain that balance—the system's status quo. This is true of cultures, organizations, institutions, and our own individual minds and hearts. This is why we naturally feel some internal resistance, some tension or anxiety, whenever we are called to change. Our balance has shifted from what we are comfortable with or used to. This tension encourages us to resist or push back against any change—even a change that we might desire, value, or need. In this way, our internal systems initially resist all change.

This resistance is instinctual and happens unconsciously. If we're not vigilant, this resistance—and the fear that accompanies it—can actually distort our critical thinking to come up with rationalizations and excuses that justify our refusal to change.

Changing a system—or even accepting change in ourselves, others, or the world—requires mindfulness, a conscious choice, and repeated positive actions. We need to be aware of our resistance and be willing to challenge it. We may also need to feel the fear behind our resistance without denying it, and then consciously choose to act according to our values.

Acceptance

Acceptance is both an ending and a beginning. It often generates renewed energy and a sense of freedom and peace. We are no longer bound by our habits, our fears, our old ideas, or our resistance; the energy that went into our defenses is now available to go into discovery and recovery.

The more we practice acceptance, the more we are able to live in—and work with—the present. We stop saying to ourselves, "If only things were different," and instead say, "What am I being called to do right now? How can I be part of the solution rather than the problem?" As Bill observed, "Once I finally accepted that good grades came from study and hard work and not some mysterious natural ability, I was able to put down the video games and pick up the books. Did I like it? Not at first, but when I got my grades and they were all As, I was proud and glad that I had accepted what I needed to do to achieve my goal."

In part, acceptance involves saying yes to the world as it is, rather than how we want or hope it to be. But it also involves accepting *ourselves* as we are right now, with all our flaws, weaknesses, and limitations—and then being willing to change them, step by step, without falling into shame and self-blame.

Acceptance is an act of stepping closer to truth and not resisting its message and direction. As my client Edwin told me, "One of the best days of my life was when I finally accepted that I had a problem with expressing anger. At last I was able to stop resisting and signed up for an anger management class. Once I had been to a couple of sessions, I wondered what I had been so afraid of and resistant about. And soon I stopped expending so much energy on blaming, justifying, and making excuses. I started to change for the better, and it felt good."

Talma's Story

Talma was a twenty-five-year-old Anishinabe woman whose name meant "crash of thunder." Her life lived up to her name. She was not just an alcoholic, but an angry *alcoholic. If someone looked directly at her when she was drunk enough, she would charge them, screaming, with her fists flying. She had been repeatedly abused as a child, and both of her parents had died of alcoholism. Her entire childhood had been very difficult and painful. But now, Talma used her childhood as an excuse for resisting any change in how she acted.*

Talma ended up in treatment for her alcoholism, and for the first three weeks she resisted and chased away everyone with her looks of rage and tone of disgust. After a while, everyone but her counselor left her alone.

After three weeks, her counselor told her, "Talma, we're recommending that you extend your stay, for it's clear that you haven't accepted your illness yet." Talma bellowed with fury and ran to her room.

Her room looked out onto a field, and standing in the field, staring at her, was a deer. Talma opened the sliding glass door and charged the deer, yelling at it, "What are you looking at?" The deer did not move. Only when she got about five feet from it did the deer turn and slowly walk away.

The next afternoon, Talma's aunt appeared at the treatment center with a package. Her aunt was a good, kind woman; she was one of the few people Talma had never yelled at. Her aunt sat her down and said, "I have something for you, and a request. I'm asking that you accept that you are Anishinabe."

Talma replied, "I do accept that. I know I'm Anishinabe. I feel it in my body and my heart."

Her aunt shook her head. "No, you're an angry alcoholic woman who lives in her wounds instead of in the community of those who love you." She handed Talma the package and said, "Last night in my dream a deer came to me and told me to bring you this."

Talma opened the package. Inside was a dancing dress.

"This was your grandmother's dancing dress," her aunt said. "She wanted your mother to have it, but her drinking killed her before she could dance. It's yours now; the deer wants you to accept that you are Anishinabe. We don't drink—we dance. Stay at this treatment center. Listen to their words. Work on your dress; make it your own. When the pain of your past comes, put on the dress and dance. Accept what and who you are. Then come home to us when you're done here." She stood up. "Either do that or burn the dress and live in your pain. I love you. Now let's go have supper."

That night it stormed, the thunder was loud, and Talma danced.

Questions for contemplation:

1. Is there some important task, challenge, or change that you have been resisting for some time? What are you afraid will happen if you stop resisting? What freedom, relief, or other positive results might occur if you stop resisting?

2. We usually think in terms of solving problems by rolling up our sleeves and fixing them, but some problems

are best solved by simply accepting how things are. Can you recall a situation in your life where things improved not because you fixed them, but because you accepted them? How did you feel when you finally came to that acceptance? How did other people respond as a result of your acceptance?

3. As of right now, where do you place yourself on the continuum from resistance to acceptance?

Resentment	Forgiveness

Resentment

Resentment means "to feel again"—and sometimes, again and again and again. When we feel wronged, we may seek refuge in resentment, but resentment never actually gives us sanctuary or peace; instead, it destroys us from the inside out. In fact, resentment is so dangerous that some people say, "Resentment is like drinking poison and waiting for the other person to die."

When we feel wronged or put down or like we've had to submit to the power of another, we may replay a mental tape of what happened, over and over, noticing all the wrongs of the other yet seeing only our own rightness and innocence. But the funny thing about resentment is that, while we might feel temporarily vindicated or superior or righteous, we don't actually feel better. In fact, we feel worse, because we've trapped ourselves in a bubble of anger and negativity.

The only antidote to resentment is to step away from it. This means letting go of our rightness and the other person's wrongness, and letting go of the past in favor of the present.

It's all too easy to become possessed by resentments. They can spread like cancer, breeding more resentment. They keep us from healing old emotional wounds. They also keep us stuck in the past (even if the past is just minutes ago) and in our own distorted memories. They pull us down into our reptilian brain.

People in recovery programs are often told that if they have resentment, they should pray for whomever they resent for thirty to ninety days. Prayer is a neocortex activity, so whenever we pray for someone, we help move our energy connected to that person from our reptilian brain to our neocortex. That energy can now be directed toward solutions rather than resentment.

Underneath resentment lies a hardened mixture of fear, sadness, and a sense of powerlessness. In his classic book *The Spirituality of Imperfection: Storytelling and the Journey to Wholeness,* Ernest Kurtz sums up the dangers of resentment beautifully: "Resentment is the refusal, out of fear, to cross the bridge of sadness and let ourselves back into the impermanent world of relationship. Anger as resentment refuses relationship, slashing at everything and everyone that comes close. But our pain can be healed only by some kind of closeness, some kind of connection with others. Sadness opens us to the need for unity and community."

Forgiveness

Forgiveness allows us to end resentment. It is a wholehearted acceptance that the past can't be changed.

Forgiveness comes in different forms. Sometimes we grant forgiveness; other times we receive it. In either case, however, forgiveness is a release, a liberation of energies. It creates healing for both the person being forgiven and the person doing the forgiving.

Forgiveness isn't only something we grant to others. When we have hurt someone else, we need to make amends and restitution, but we also need to forgive ourselves, whether or not others forgive us. But self-forgiveness only comes from a true willingness to change our actions and attitudes.

We forgive the past by not continually repeating the past. Forgiveness comes from learning the lessons we need to learn in order to end this repetition. In this way, forgiveness is often the last part of healing an old wound.

We are all flawed, all imperfect—and we all make mistakes. Forgiveness enables us to release ourselves and others from our pain and fears, to grow closer, and to continue on together. This is why forgiveness is such an important and powerful positive Spiritual Principle—because it preserves relationships.

When we forgive either others or ourselves, we rise above instinctual limitations. For a time—sometimes just moments, sometimes longer—we experience peace, serenity, and release. We let go of self-centeredness and ego, two key ingredients of resentment. As a result, new opportunities for growth and connection appear, and our minds and hearts are reset to a gentler, kinder rhythm.

Mikhail's Story

My client Mikhail told me this story:

"It was a Tuesday, late in the afternoon. I was tired, angry, and lonely. For years, I had walked around full of anger, bitterness, rage, and resentment. I was sitting on a park bench when Martha, my ex-wife, walked up and sat down beside me.

"Martha and I had been married for nine years. One day, in a drunken, coked-up rage, she walked out the door, saying she couldn't take it anymore. I had not seen her in six years. She was the only woman I ever loved, and when she walked out that door, I retreated further into the bitterness and anger that had helped chase her away.

"What was she doing here? What did she want? Martha asked if we could talk. Reluctantly, I said yes. She started to cry and said, 'I have something to say to you.' With that, she pulled out a list and started describing in detail all the mean things she had ever done to me. The time she passed out at my work Christmas party. The names she had called me. The things she

had thrown at me. The list went on and on through dozens of items, including things I had long forgotten about, and others I had never known about or realized.

"I kept waiting for her to blame me, for that is what we had done for years—used each other as our excuse for inflicting hurts. But she didn't.

"She went on for fifteen minutes, crying and describing in detail all the things she had done. When she was finished, she asked what I would need from her in order to forgive her for the harm she had caused me.

"I knew in my heart that if I were to list all the wrongs I had done to her, the list would be just as long. So I asked her, 'Why are you doing this?'

"She explained that four years ago, she had gone through treatment for her cocaine and alcohol addiction, and it was now time for her to try to heal some of the wounds she had created during her years of addiction. I had no idea what to think or say. Finally, I asked, 'Why do you want my forgiveness?' She wasn't totally sure, she said, but she knew that she needed it.

"By now anger and adrenaline were rushing through me. I said, 'You know what you can do for me? You can leave me the hell alone. I never want to see your face again. If you do that, then I'll forgive you.'

"With tears running down her cheeks, she thanked me for the good things I had done for her—helping her through school, being there when her mother died, caring about her when no one else would, planting the seed that told her she needed to get help, and so on.

"Then she stood up and said, 'I'll be going now. Not to worry—if my disappearing is what will help you heal from the bad things I've done, I'll never bother you again. Thank you; you always were a good man and a good husband. The marriage didn't work because of me, not you. Thank you for the love you gave me. I don't think I'd be alive today without it.' And with that she turned and walked away.

"That was three years ago. I wish I hadn't sent her away that day. Recently, I heard through a mutual friend that she is doing well—still clean and sober, working at a local bank. She's now remarried and living across town. She has kept her promise not to contact me. But some day soon I plan to call her and seek her forgiveness for the way I treated her in the park that afternoon."

Questions for contemplation:

1. Are you presently carrying any resentments inside you? If so, in what way are those resentments helping or hindering you? How do you think you would feel if you were able to let go of each of these resentments? What would enable you to let go of each one?

2. Think of a time when you experienced someone else's forgiveness. How did you feel when you received it? How did it change your relationship with that person? How did it change your life from then on? How did it affect your willingness to forgive yourself?

3. As of right now, where do you place yourself on the continuum from resentment to forgiveness?

Control	Surrender

Control

Control tries to solve problems not through collaboration or creativity or negotiation or compromise, but through domination. It relies on raw power, not ethical power. Control thus never promotes healing, and it often creates wounds.

Control is about the submission of others to our will and desires. Control attempts to make others smaller or powerless so that our reptilian brain can feel bigger, safer, more powerful, more comfortable, and less afraid. In fact, however, any attempt to control others only reveals our own fear. Rarely do controlling people see that they are seeking domination. Typically, controlling people only see their own rightness. Paradoxically, people who try to control others are actually out of control themselves. Instinctual forces rather than positive Spiritual Principles are leading them.

As controlling behaviors within relationships increase, communication becomes a casualty. Words are now used as weapons or used to set traps, instead of to find or create meaning. Words and tones become aggressive; they are used to push others into their own instinctual reptilian brains, where they are much easier to manipulate. Communication is now a vehicle used to create power struggles.

Surrender

Surrender is the process of allowing ourselves to serve and follow positive Spiritual Principles. It is a release from self, from ego, from instinct. In this release, our desires become unimportant.

Surrender involves letting go of *my truth* for *a truth*, and an acceptance that we are not in control of life. Only then do we open up to a new life, new relationships, new opportunities, new ideas, and new ways of seeing the world.

Surrender is the first step in the process of transformation. It can be worked toward, but it can't be willed, for it takes place mainly in the unconscious.

Surrender is usually born out of hard times. In our initial moments of surrender, we are often exposed, vulnerable, and aware of our incompleteness. These moments can feel like an act of contraction, a loss, or a defeat. But soon afterward, an expansion occurs. We step into vastness and ever-expanding qualities that we hadn't seen (or had ignored) before our surrender. Options start to appear.

Surrender is not submission, a giving up of power. Instead, it is an admission that we do not have the power to resolve a dilemma or create the results we desire. Surrender is thus an act of humility and a state of relief. Regular spiritual surrender can be our best protection against willfulness and an inflated ego.

Surrender involves choice; it is an act of free will, even though we may feel we have no other option.

Rashid's Story

Rashid always had to be right.

When he and Terri met in college, they clicked immediately. His high self-confidence and assertiveness complemented her shyness. They got married soon after graduation.

But Rashid's rightness and assertiveness soon started to take a toll on Terri and the marriage. Even when he was wrong, Rashid had to be right. He was always pushing her, even about small things. "Why are you wearing that dress? The blue one looks so much better on you." "Didn't your mother teach you the proper way to hold a fork?" "What makes you think you know anything about gardening?" He often corrected Terri and told her what he felt she should think.

Two years into their marriage, Rashid's job was cut back from full time to part time. To make ends meet, Terri took a job as an administrative assistant at a new technology company.

To her own and Rashid's surprise, Terri quickly became a rising star in the fast-growing company. Her insights and skills saw the organization through a couple of critical transitions, and within eighteen months it became very successful and went public.

The president of the company offered Terri a job as one of five new vice presidents. The job would triple her salary and give her generous stock options. She would now be making quite a bit more than Rashid.

That night she excitedly told Rashid about the job offer. To her shock, his first reaction was, "Well, you're not going to take the job, are you? The moment the company has financial trouble, you'll be downsized to save money—but they'll probably keep all the administrative assistants." Nothing could have hurt her more than that response.

Terri started to cry. After about twenty minutes, she took out a suitcase and started packing it. She said to her husband, "Honey, I'm taking that job and I'm leaving you. I'm going to get an apartment, and I'll give you four months. If you can't find a way for me to be equal with you, and to have a life of my own, we're through. I love you, I always have, but you've become a scared little man. You can either enjoy my success with me or live your life without me." She kissed him on the cheek and left.

For three weeks, Rashid came home from work and just sat in the dark house. He knew Terri was right, but he had no idea what to do. He lost fifteen pounds just sitting in his chair staring out into the blank room, hoping Terri would return.

Late one night, Rashid broke down crying. All the fear and pain from the decades of having to be right boiled over. He got on his knees and started praying. It was a screaming prayer: "Help me! Tell me what to do!"

For forty minutes, Rashid sobbed on his knees. When his crying stopped, he knew what to do: call his wife and ask for her help.

He picked up the phone and dialed her cell number. "Hello?" she said sleepily. "Terri," he said, his voice catching, "I'm so sorry. You're right—and I've been so wrong." He started crying again, and Terri cried with him.

That night, after years of trying to control other people, Rashid surrendered.

In the weeks that followed, Rashid found a good counselor and started the process of becoming a better man. Together, he and Terri were able to create a new marriage.

From that night on, whenever they went anywhere together by car, Terri would drive. It was their ongoing symbol of Rashid's surrender.

Questions for contemplation:

1. Is there anyone in your life—your partner, your kids, your parents, your in-laws, your friends—to whom you relate by trying to manage and control them? Why do you feel this is necessary? What do you think would happen if you let go of this control?

2. Think of a time in your life when you let go and experienced surrender. How did you feel at the time? How has your life changed as a result of your surrender? How has

your surrender affected others? Is there an aspect of your life now where you feel you may need to surrender?

3. As of right now, where do you place yourself on the continuum from control to surrender?

atlanta-fulton public library system

Milton Branch
404.613.4402
www.afpls.org

Checked Out Items 1/19/2016 16:35
XXXXXX0370

m Title	Due Date
2002630735	2/16/2016
rawing for everyone : classic and eative fundamentals	
2002517668	2/16/2016
/hat matters most is how well you walk rough the fire	
2002570097	2/16/2016
encil magic : surprisingly simple echniques for color and graphic pencils	
2002579999	2/16/2016
inding your moral compass : ansformative principles to guide you in ecovery and life	
R2001918719	2/16/2016
\stronomy	
R2001917968	2/16/2016
\stronomy : a self-teaching guide	
R2001994736	2/16/2016
he art of colored pencil drawing	
R2001971601	2/16/2016
he art of drawing painting portraits	

355 Mayfield Rd.

Have a great day!

Arrogance   **Humility**

Arrogance

Knowing our strengths and limitations, and operating from that knowledge, creates both self-confidence and humility.

Arrogance is the lack of this knowledge—an exaggerated, distorted view of who we are, what we know, and what we are capable of. Arrogant people may also have a distorted view of what they feel they deserve or are entitled to.

Arrogant people often seek to be untouchable. They are often alone and treat their loneliness as badge of courage. Randy's comments demonstrate this: "The reason I have few friends is others' fear of my intelligence. When they're around me, they get tired of being wrong." Yet arrogance is essentially a lie, because it rejects reality in favor of a false view of ourselves. Worst of all, arrogance stifles spiritual growth, because it won't allow us to say some of the most important sentences in life: "I was wrong," "I'm sorry," and "Please help me."

Humility

Acquiring greater humility is the central theme of spiritual growth. Truths always lead us back to humility—to how little we know and how much we can learn. Humility is protective. Without humility, we can easily fall back into instinctual reactions.

Humility binds us to positive Spiritual Principles, especially during times of adversity and times of doubt. The more humility we possess, the stronger the bond we have with these Principles.

Our instinctual side experiences humility as a loss of power instead of an avenue to ethical power. It sees humility as humiliation or weakness or submission. Yet humility is actually one of the most direct roads to ethical power. When we are humble, we see our imperfections as roads to the Divine.

Humility both creates and is the result of correct perspective. Through humble eyes, we see the suffering of the world. Through humble eyes, we see how our own limitations create a need—and an opening—for others. Through humble eyes, we see that all things are connected, interwoven, interdependent.

Humility creates willingness and spiritual freedom, enabling us to heal what we can, learn what we can, and be of service wherever there is a need.

Herb's Story

Herb had been a professor at the same university for twenty-nine years. He was tired—tired of the students, their predictable questions, their fears, and their obsession with grades. "God, what I would give for a student who cared about knowledge and not their damn GPA!"

When new, young professors would challenge Herb and stand up for students, he would say, "You wait and see if you're not as sick of them as I am after you've been here twenty-nine years." Herb often told his colleagues how much he looked forward to retirement, which was only six years away.

In class, Herb sometimes mocked and insulted students who asked questions that he thought were naïve or simple-minded. He had fifty different ways of telling people how little he *thought of their ideas. His students quickly learned not to ask questions.*

Early in his career, Herb had published a book that had received much praise, and Herb was still feeding off that apple. It was required reading in all his classes, even the ones where reading it served little or no purpose.

Herb had a wife and two grown children, all of whom had learned to pay no attention to his rants about his students, other professors, the government, or even just what was on the news that night.

One winter night, everything suddenly changed for Herb. He was arrested for soliciting a prostitute.

Herb's world quickly fell apart. His picture was placed on the city's convicted johns website. His wife used it as her ticket out of the marriage. The university dismissed him, citing the moral clause in his contract. Both of Herb's children told him they wanted little to do with him.

Finally, with his old life gone and his secret world exposed, Herb found some humility. He began to see a counselor, to whom he explained, "I loved going out, finding hookers on the street, and having sex with them. It was the only thing in my life that made me feel alive. When I was out on the street look-ing for the ladies, I finally felt like I could breathe.

"It's sad to think that the only place I felt alive was out on those streets looking for women to pay for quick sex, especially when I had so much liveliness around me—all my students, the university, my wife, my own kids." Herb had to lose every-thing—especially his own arrogance—to find humility and see what was really important in life.

Questions for contemplation:

1. In what times and places are you most likely to become arrogant? What about this arrogance feels good to you? What do you do if someone challenges you when you're

feeling and acting arrogant? In what ways does this arrogance help you? How does it hurt you? How does it hurt others?

2. Think back to a moment in your life when you were deeply humbled. Did you embrace humility or resist it? What effects did being humbled have on you? On others around you? Are there any areas of your life that you need to bring more humility to now?

3. As of right now, where do you place yourself on the continuum from arrogance to humility?

Intolerance

Intolerance is a refusal to respect or make room for people, groups, ideas, and opinions that differ from those we identify with. It is the sibling of arrogance (the two often hang out together) and a cousin of hate, unkindness, self-righteousness, ignorance, and unmanaged fear.

On the surface, intolerance appears to make an enemy of whomever it considers the "other." In fact, however, intolerance's biggest enemy—what it fears and despises most—is truth. And what intolerance most embraces are negative "-isms": cynicism, racism, sexism, ageism, conformism, sensationalism, fundamentalism, moralism, nihilism. Each of these -isms is a form of moral decay—a decay that intolerant people project onto others and refuse to acknowledge in themselves.

Radical fundamentalism is intolerance in its purest and most dangerous form. It offers us a stark and simple choice: We can submit ourselves to the will of a particular group, dogma, or leader, and go to heaven; or we can deserve to be murdered, to go to hell, or both. Radical fundamentalism thus promotes submission to other human beings in the name of surrender to a Higher Power.

Among its leaders, radical fundamentalism encourages intense narcissism and a lust for power and domination. Among its followers, however, radical fundamentalism encourages fear and a lack of thought, discernment, and self-esteem. As Erich Fromm wrote in *The Heart of Man*, "The majority of men are suggestible, half awake children, willing to surrender their will to anyone who speaks with a voice that is threatening or sweet enough to sway them." Radical fundamentalism thus appeals to people who have failed to create genuinely spiritual lives. In fact, the farther away we are from authentic intimate relationships and positive Spiritual Principles, the more susceptible we are to fundamentalism.

The power of positive Spiritual Principles is the power to create and the power to transform. The power of radical fundamentalism, however—the one and only power it has—is the power to destroy. At its heart, radical fundamentalism is thus the expression of impotence through acts of destruction.

Tolerance

Many worlds exist within this world. Some we find comfort in, some we are curious about, some scare us, and some disgust us. We may not like or appreciate them all, but we can learn from them all.

Tolerance is not about embracing or honoring every person and idea. It is simply about acknowledging the existence of each and allowing them to coexist with us. We don't give up our own seat at the table, but we don't demand that anyone else give up their seat, either. There is room for all.

Tolerance slows us down so we can experience and learn from ideas, customs, cultures, and people who differ from us. As we learn, we develop curiosity, empathy, and compassion. Tolerance thus creates a very important protective barrier between us and hatred.

Tolerance isn't about being naïve; a tolerant person doesn't condone or accept the harming of others. Tolerance does, however, accept that there is evil in the world and in our hearts—and that, in the face of this evil, our job is always to work to do the next right thing.

Luke's Story

As Luke grew up, he was taught that homosexuality was a sin and that gay people will go to hell. He took these ideas to heart because he wanted to be a good human being and a good Christian.

As an adult, Luke continued to follow the Christianity he had been raised with. He volunteered at his church, delivered meals to shut-ins on weekends, kept his yard looking nice, and was friendly to his neighbors. When his wife died, Luke's faith was temporarily shaken, but his minister assured him that Arianna was in heaven with the angels, permanently separated from thieves, murderers, rapists, unbelievers, and gays.

Luke's big problem was that his son, Judd, was gay.

This first became clear when Judd was a young teenager. Luke took Judd to a counselor at his church to have him "cured," but this only put distance between Judd and his parents.

Believing that Judd was headed for hell, Luke did everything he could to "fix" him. He pushed Judd to excel in sports, took Judd hunting, and did all the things Luke believed would set his son right. This led to many heated arguments between the two.

Once when Judd was fourteen, Luke caught him looking at a gay Internet dating site. He slapped his son across the face and shouted, "Do you want to go to hell?"

The day after Judd graduated from high school, Luke found this note on the kitchen table:

> Dad,
> I can't argue with you anymore about this. I've changed my cell phone number. I won't be a burden or a source of shame to you anymore.
> Love, your gay son,
> Judd

Luke was crushed; he had lost his wife, and now he had lost his son, too.

Eight years later, Luke received a note in the mail from Judd. In it, Judd explained that he was doing well, had a good career, and was married to Keith, his high school sweetheart (Luke had met him and had thought he was a nice guy). They had adopted a son, Allen. There was no return address.

It was then that Luke started to see that what he thought was love was actually a mixture of love and other things: fear, falsehoods, and intolerance. Each day Luke would read the letter again and tears would come to his eyes.

After about a year, Luke decided to hire a detective to locate his son. It took her only a few days to find Judd's address in a city two states away.

Luke sent Judd this simple letter:

Judd,

I don't know what to do, but I know I'm the one in the wrong here. Please call; the number is the same. I never changed it, hoping you would call. If you can forgive me, I'd like to talk, but mainly I'll listen. I'd love to meet Keith and my grandson, Allen.

Love, the father of a gay son,
Luke

Questions for contemplation:

1. Is there some person, group, or idea that you are intolerant of? What about this person, group, or idea scares or bothers you? Why? Knowing that you don't have the power to change anyone except yourself, what can you change about your own thinking? What can you do that might make you less bothered or afraid?

2. Have you ever been in a situation where some person or group couldn't tolerate your existence because of your

age, gender, race, social class, nationality, religion, political views, or sexual orientation? When you feel intolerance bubbling up in you, do you recall how it felt to be on the receiving end of someone else's intolerance?

3. As of right now, where do you place yourself on the continuum from intolerance to tolerance?

Despair	Hope

Despair

Despair is to our situation what shame is to ourselves. It is a feeling that our circumstances are both unbearable and unchangeable—that our life is and always will be dark and miserable.

Despair is like a black hole in our soul. It steals energy from both the present and the future and drains it away. Over time, our self-confidence, self-esteem, and hope can get drained away as well.

Despair can be seductive. It can feed on itself, typically by telling us that we are a victim, or a pawn of others, or even a martyr. Or it can tell us that there is nothing special about us—that we are just part of the poor, helpless masses who mean nothing. Either way, the biggest danger of despair is that it encourages us to find some identity and pleasure in suffering instead of values.

Despair refuses to accept the fact that everything changes; that nothing (except perhaps death) is permanent; and that, when we feel helpless, a power greater than us can restore us to sanity, if we allow ourselves to embrace positive Spiritual Principles.

Hope

Hope is an awareness that care and love can and will exist in the future, and that our challenges, while significant, are not insurmountable. It is the belief that dawn will follow the dark night of our soul.

Hope is also the practice of staying vulnerable, open, and connected to positive Spiritual Principles, especially during times of adversity. Hope is thus not just a feeling and an awareness, but an activity.

All positive Spiritual Principles have a bit of hope—a small amount of light—embedded in them; collectively, they create a beacon of hope, and the stronger our relationships with positive Spiritual Principles become, the brighter that beacon becomes as well.

Hope is a natural by-product of living a moral life and a reservoir of spiritual energy that can keep us going during difficult times. It is also a creative force that seeks to connect us with something greater than ourselves.

One of the major functions of hope is to put some distance between ourselves and our instinctual fears. It responds to "I might fail" with "It's okay to fail; try anyway. If you fail, learn from it and try again!" It responds to "I don't know what will happen" with "You can't succeed unless you try." And it responds to "I'm afraid" with "Go ahead and feel afraid. But do the next right thing anyway."

Gabrielle's Story

When Gabrielle was growing up, her home was a place of danger and fear. Her mother was an addict who worked as a prostitute. Gabrielle had never met her father. Gabrielle's mother often brought her tricks home at night. They were loud and often drunk or high.

One night, when Gabrielle was ten, she woke up to see one of her mother's tricks standing in her bedroom doorway, playing with his zipper. She screamed as loud as she could, and he turned and walked down the hall. From then on, she slept with a kitchen knife under her pillow.

One evening, as Gabrielle walked home from a friend's house, she heard singing coming from a church. She went inside, sat down in back, and listened to the choir practicing. The music was beautiful and peaceful, and it made her feel happy, calm, and safe.

The minister, who was working late, noticed her and sat down next to her. Gabrielle asked him what she would need to do to be part of the choir. He said simply, "Be part of the church and come to choir practices."

The next Sunday, Gabrielle came to the service to hear the choir sing. Two Sundays later, she returned. She kept returning on most Sunday mornings, and within a few months, she began singing in the choir.

Gabrielle's home life didn't improve; in fact, her mother was diagnosed with diabetes. By the time Gabrielle was fourteen, she had called 911 three times after she came home to find her mother in insulin shock.

Her mother continued to turn tricks for a living. But one night, with tears in her eyes, she said to Gabrielle, "Honey, I'm so glad you're going to church and that you're putting together a life different than mine. Now, if you really want to do better than me—and I want you to—you'll need to get good grades in school, too."

Gabrielle had never really thought much about school either way. She had done just enough to get by but no more, earning mostly Cs and an occasional B. Several of her teachers had told her that she could do much better if only she tried, but until now, she hadn't seen any reason to try.

Beginning in eighth grade, with her mother's urging, her minister's blessing, and some tutoring from two members of her church choir, Gabrielle took school seriously. Soon she was earning mostly As and an occasional B—and, to her shock, her mom told her for the first time that she was proud of her.

Gabrielle's mother never was able to put together a good life for herself; she never became a reliable and nurturing mother. But she did come to Gabrielle's high school graduation and, with tears in her eyes, gave her a leather briefcase with her initials on it as a graduation gift.

Gabrielle went on to college on a scholarship, then to graduate school. She became a medical researcher. Today, at age thirty-two, she still sings in the church choir and is tutoring a teenage girl named Isabella.

Questions for contemplation:

1. Think about the last time you fell into despair. In retrospect, was your despair justified? Was there anything you could have done to improve either your situation or your response to it?

2. Think of someone who gives you hope. Now think of something you've done yourself that gives you hope. What do these two examples of hope have in common? What does this common thread suggest about keeping hope alive for you in the future?

3. As of right now, where do you place yourself on the continuum from despair to hope?

Indifference   Compassion

Indifference

Indifference is a complete lack of interest and concern regarding things outside our sphere of control. It is our instinctual side ignoring everything outside of its tiny personal territory.

Indifference is also a form of narcissism, because it declares, "Unless it relates to me, it's not on my radar screen." This is how, in Nazi Germany, people walked past Auschwitz on their way to the market, thinking little of the people inside or of the smoke rising out of the chimneys.

Indifference responds to positive Spiritual Principles with "So what?" and to their calls with "Whatever." Thus, indifference can help negative spiritual principles to gain a foothold and, over time, to begin to take over our life.

Indifference to the suffering and joys of others is a characteristic of our reptilian brain, which is interested only in its own personal pleasure and survival. We can easily snap out of indifference, however, by imagining ourselves in another's shoes—thus reprocessing the information through our neocortex, where empathy resides.

Compassion

Compassion combines the active sharing of another's suffering with reaching out to help that person heal and move forward.

It is the smile of a friend as we talk about our mistakes, the laughter and tears of a self-help group as we tell our story, and the loving touch of a parent comforting a frightened or confused child. More than many positive Spiritual Principles, compassion has the power to heal spiritual wounds and soften a hardened heart.

A mother sent her daughter to the store to get some milk. When the young girl came home a bit late, the mother asked her what had taken her so long. The little girl said, "I was on my way home when I came across a girl whose doll was broken." The mother asked, "Did you stop to help her fix it?" The daughter said, "No, I stopped to help her cry."

Compassion asks that we make friends with our flaws and faults, for the further we go down the spiritual path, the more we come to know how limited and imperfect we all are.

Compassion is born out of our weakness and suffering—yet it contains immense power. It also releases us from suffering, whether we give compassion or receive it.

Gladys and Hans's Story

Two elderly strangers were seated side by side on a flight from Chicago to New York. Hans was of German descent; Gladys was British. After spending most of the flight in silence, they engaged in a few minutes of small talk and discovered that they were both on their way to visit their middle-aged children.

As the plane began its descent, Hans asked Gladys about her husband. "He was killed long ago," she said softly, "in the Second World War, during one of the bombings of London. I still miss him and think of him every day."

She looked over at Hans, who had removed a handkerchief from his pocket and had begun to dab at his eyes. "What about your wife?" she asked.

Hans looked back at her and said, with his voice shaking, "She was killed in the Allied bombing of Dresden."

They both sighed, and Gladys removed a tissue from her purse. There was a moment of awkward silence, and then, together, they both said softly, "I'm sorry."

Questions for contemplation:

1. Think back to a time when your indifference transformed into compassion. What events led up to that transformation? What did you learn as a result? How has your life been different since then?

2. When was the last time someone treated you with great compassion? What did they do? How did you feel and respond? What did you learn from that encounter?

3. As of right now, where do you place yourself on the continuum from indifference to compassion?

Irresponsibility	Accountability

Irresponsibility

Irresponsibility asks others to handle things that only we should (or can) handle. Irresponsibility thus combines selfishness, laziness, and thoughtlessness in a single package.

Irresponsibility comes in many different forms: not taking care of things you need to take care of, pretending you can do more than you actually can, pretending you can't do as much as you actually can, and refusing to be accountable to positive Spiritual Principles. Appetites, passions, aspirations, pride, ambition—all of these pull at us to be selfish and irresponsible.

We're responsible not just for what we say and do, but for the spirit and tone in which we say and do it—our attitudes, demeanor, body language, inflections, and so on. If we say the right words in an angry or annoyed tone, then we've been irresponsible because we haven't looked after all the important aspects of our communication.

Irresponsibility urges us to blame others and put distance between them and us. In practice, however, this only creates more consequences for us. Furthermore, each act of irresponsibility makes us spiritually smaller and reduces our ethical power.

It's easy to become deliberately irresponsible, especially when we're afraid. But it's easier still to become unwittingly irresponsible through a simple lack of care or attention. This is why it's important to monitor—and regularly inventory—our actions, words, decisions, and attitudes.

One common form of irresponsibility is underperformance. By routinely doing less—or less well—than we are capable of, we train others to lower their expectations of us. They come to see us as responsible but mediocre rather than capable but irresponsible. This arrangement may fool others, but when we practice it, we shortchange ourselves, the people who depend on us, and the Divine within us.

Accountability

We do not often get to choose what happens to us, but we do get to choose how we respond to it.

Like it or not, each of us is continuously responsible for making choices. Sometimes these choices are limited, painful, or difficult to make. Accountability is the willingness to make these choices and accept their consequences in our flawed and uncertain world. It ties us to our conscience, keeps us in our neocortex, and requires us to consider what consequences our actions may have.

Irresponsibility asks us to believe that we are merely victims and pawns, and thus entitled to treat others badly. Accountability tells us that we are always responsible to ourselves and others for our words, deeds, attitudes, and intentions, no matter what we may feel and no matter what our circumstances may be.

When your partner asks you to change the way you treat one of his family members, you may feel an urge to get defensive. Do you follow that urge, or do you decide to discuss the matter instead of reacting?

When you're driving down the road and see that two cars have just collided, creating a twisted mass of metal, do you drive on past? Or do you stop to help, not knowing what you'll find?

When your brother asks you to attend a fundraiser for a cause you don't believe in, what do you tell him? Are you respectful and honest in your explanation?

These are all moments of accountability.

Accountability is not theoretical. It is practiced in real-life situations, and it involves specific actions and other flesh-and-blood human beings. It also involves asking ourselves, and answering, some tough questions: *What should I choose? What type of partner am I? How should I conduct myself right now?*

Whenever we choose accountability over irresponsibility, we make the moment holy.

Summer's Story

When my niece, Summer, was young, she often tried to seem big and tough. But in her actions, she was often irresponsible. She wouldn't always do what she promised (or needed) to do, and she would sometimes blame others for failures, or play the role of victim, or act less capable than she actually was.

I often challenged Summer with questions about account-ability: "Are you part of the problem, or are you part of the solu-tion?" She would usually roll her eyes at me, though sometimes she'd also give me a bit of a smile.

Summer's attitude changed dramatically when, in her twenties, she gave birth to my wonderful grandniece Katelin. Suddenly she had to be accountable 24/7. One moment of irresponsibility could cause Katelin to get hurt. Summer was in love with her daughter and wanted to be a good mom. She quickly learned that this meant caring well for her daughter, fulfilling each commitment she made, and not blaming others for her own mistakes and failures.

One day a couple of years ago, Summer pulled me aside. She said, "Uncle, I've got something to show you," and rolled up her sleeve. Her inner arm was tattooed with two small letters, "S/P"—standing for Solution/Problem, she told me. She smiled and said, "I decided I'll be part of the solution."

Earlier this year I had "S/P" tattooed on my hand to express solidarity with my niece for our journey together. These two letters of accountability are like having my conscience tattooed on my hand.

Questions for contemplation:

1. Think of an incident in your life in which you acted irresponsibly. What were you trying to avoid? What emotions did you feel at the time? How did your irresponsibility ultimately affect others? If you were faced with the same situation now, what would you do differently?

2. Do you want the other people in your life to be accountable to you? Do you feel you have been sufficiently accountable to them? Are there any positive Spiritual Principles to which you would like to be more accountable? What can you do right now, or very soon, to start being more accountable to them?

3. As of right now, where do you place yourself on the continuum from irresponsibility to accountability?

Hate	Love

Hate

"I never feel so alive as when I'm hating someone or something," my client Sheila told me. "When I'm caught up in hate, my body radiates energy and heat."

When we hate, we can feel so justified, so entitled, so clear, so privileged, so righteous, and so very alive. This is because hate gives great energy to our reptilian brain.

At the same time, however, hate encourages us to embrace irresponsibility, because we never feel responsible to or for the things we hate. We feel free of conscience and free of any consequences. In fact, however, the only things we are genuinely free from are positive Spiritual Principles and our own values.

Hate is a trance state, a form of intoxication. It is also a powerful binding agent. People with the same hatreds often bind together to share, justify, and heighten their trance. This trance can easily feel like strength, but it is actually a combination of delusion and impotence.

Hate tries to gain a sense of power by destroying things—destroying the moment, destroying the mood, destroying a family, destroying a building, destroying the person who feels the hate. But these actions don't actually create any power—only violence.

Love

Love is not an intense liking, longing, or attraction. It is a form of giving, of openness, of vulnerability, and of service.

Love is active; it exists only within relationships. It involves letting go, not holding on; sacrificing, not acquiring; and faith, not certainty. Love asks that we give more and more of ourselves to others, to positive Spiritual Principles, and to the Divine. It helps us to transcend our instincts and to transform our passion into service and spiritual growth.

The more we develop our capacity to love, the better we become at finding meaning, solving complex personal and spiritual problems, healing deep wounds, and building intimate relationships.

Paige's Story

Paige knew the world was very dangerous. Her parents had proven that to her by the time she was six, after they had beaten her for the thirtieth time. Both her parents had personality disorders, and they spent much of their time at war with each other. Paige, their only child, was a casualty of their war. She spent her early life trapped between the walls of their rage and hate.

Paige learned early on to spend as little time at home as possible. At age eleven, she began hanging out at the bowling alley and pool hall. By the time she was fifteen, she had built a reputation as a fighter who wouldn't stop swinging until either she or the other person couldn't move.

Her proudest night was the night she turned sixteen. That night she went home high on crystal meth and got in a fight with her father. She won, knocking him out with an ashtray. She got kicked out of the house for that.

She was on her own at last. She lived with friends until she met Diego, a member of the Banditos, and soon became his lady. She felt safe with Diego; he promised to protect her and did so on many occasions. But she also felt that she could protect herself when she needed to.

When she was eighteen, she forgot to take her birth control pills for a few days and became pregnant. When she told Diego, thinking he might be pleased, or at worst concerned, he went crazy. He shouted at her, called her a bitch and whore, and beat her. Then he handed her over to the other gang members, who gang-raped her and beat her some more.

When Paige finally made it to the hospital, she was close to death. She spent two weeks there, recovering. Miraculously, she hadn't lost the baby. She decided to leave the state and moved to Oregon, where she got a job at a paper mill.

The day her baby was born, Paige was changed forever. She had hoped for a boy, knowing how dangerous the world was for girls, but she gave birth to a healthy little girl.

When the nurse brought her daughter to her and asked her what her name would be, Paige said, "I don't know. I think I'll just hold her for a while, and then maybe I'll know."

As she stared into her daughter's eyes, love and caring gripped her heart. Paige started to cry. Then a voice in her head said, "It will be okay. You will be a good mother. Find a teacher to help you. I've given Grace to you so you can finally know joy and love."

When the nurse came in a few moments later, Paige told her, "My daughter's name is Grace." Then Paige told the nurse her story and asked her if there was a place where she could learn to be a good mother.

The next day the nurse brought in the hospital social worker. Together, the three of them worked out a plan for Paige and Grace. That night, Paige's hate and rage began to be transformed into a determination to love and raise her daughter well.

Paige did not become a perfect mother, of course, but she became a good and loving one. Day by day, year by year, she let go of her hate and her past. Life as a single mother was often difficult, but she never stopped loving and caring for Grace.

Until Grace turned seventeen, she never learned Paige's history; all she knew was her mother's love.

Questions for contemplation:

1. Think of a time when you hated someone. Did that hatred feel good or seductive in any way? Did it fill a need? If you no longer hate this person, what enabled you to transform or let go of that hate? If you still hate this person, what can you do now to let go of or transform that feeling?

2. Hate is an emotion, but love is an activity, an expression of connection. Can you list ten loving things—whether large or small, planned or spontaneous—that you did in the past week? What are three loving things you can do in the next twenty-four hours?

3. As of right now, where do you place yourself on the continuum from hate to love?

Self-Centeredness	Service

Self-Centeredness

In its most naked, basic, reptilian-brain form, self-centeredness is the belief that the only important things in the world are us, our possessions, our beliefs, our causes, our interests, and the people we approve of.

In day-to-day life, self-centeredness can take a variety of forms:

- a belief that we can (or should) control things

- a belief that we are somehow more important than others

- a belief that we are somehow *less* important than others (focused on what we feel makes us special, but in a negative way)

- an obsession with how others see us or think of us

- an initial internal response of *How does this affect me?* to almost every situation

- an approach to life that centers on the question *What can I get out of this?*

- a continuous "me vs. them" mentality

- an obsession with our flaws and shortcomings

Self-centeredness is nothing more than our instinctual side looking out for itself. But it hinders our ability to be intimate, to serve, to care, to empathize, and to love. We hurt others without seeing the damage our self-absorption has caused. Strangely, it even hinders our ability to love ourselves.

We're all born self-centered, and we'll all continue to have self-centered impulses until we die. But there's a vast difference between having such impulses and mindlessly—or greedily—following them.

Service

As humans, our purpose is to be of service. It is through service that our spirits bond with the spirits of others.

Service promotes healing, and creates and spreads joy. Yet it demands nothing in return; it is provided freely and without any expectation of gain. Service doesn't need to be grand; it can be as simple as shoveling the snow off a neighbor's driveway, visiting a sick friend, donating to a charity, or cleaning out the coffee pots after a community meeting.

Service pulls us out of ourselves, into relationships, and into the world. In the process, we learn what to do and what not to do, what usually works and what usually doesn't. Service is thus a wonderful learning tool.

The more we live according to positive Spiritual Principles, the more we practice and are naturally drawn to service, because service is the heart of practical spirituality. Instinct asks, *What can I get from the world?* Service asks, *What can I give to the world?* Ego tries to blind us to the needs of others; service opens our eyes to those needs and recognizes them as opportunities.

Ashley and Amy's Story

Ashley and Amy were identical twins who had very different ways of interacting with the world. One day when they were sixteen, they watched a television program about homeless people. They began talking about the issue and decided they would both volunteer with local charities.

Amy called the woman who ran the local food pantry and offered to volunteer. The director asked Amy what she had in mind. Amy said, "Whatever you need. I'm a good typist; I can use Excel; and I speak decent Spanish. But I can just sort or bag groceries if that's what you want me to do." The director replied, "Well, we had to let our janitor go because of a lack of funds; how are your skills with a mop and a broom?" Amy replied, "They're good. When do I start?"

Ashley took a different approach. She started looking for charity work that would look good on her college applications. She decided the local hospice would look best, so she called and offered to read to patients and talk with them. The volunteer coordinator replied, "Thanks very much, but right now we have plenty of volunteers for that. What we really need is someone who can help us in the laundry. You can't imagine how much laundry we do each day. We also need someone to help unpack and stock supplies. How do either of those sound?"

"No, thanks," Ashley said. "I'm more of a people person."

Questions for contemplation:

1. Recall a recent incident in which you simultaneously felt a self-centered impulse and an impulse to serve. Which impulse won out? What did you do as a result? What were the consequences of your actions? Are you glad you made the choice you did?

2. Can you list five ways in which people recently served you? Five ways in which you recently served others?

(List only the activities that people did willingly and without being paid.) For each example of service, how was someone's life affected in a specific, positive way?

3. As of right now, where do you place yourself on the continuum from self-centeredness to service?

| Disrespect | Respect |

Disrespect

Disrespect involves discounting or dehumanizing others. It can take innumerable forms. Some examples include the following:

- A friend asks for our opinion but pays no attention to what we say.

- A customer is rude and demanding to a sales clerk.

- We leave our dirty dishes in the sink for our housemate to deal with.

- We accidentally bump into someone on the sidewalk but don't apologize for it.

- We don't pick up after our dog.

When we're disrespectful, we put emotional distance between others and ourselves. As a couples counselor, I've watched many relationships fail when disrespect takes hold of a relationship. Partners stop listening to each other, and the nurturing that is so essential to a healthy relationship is lost.

When we're disrespectful, we're usually operating from a fantasy about how we believe others (or the world) should be.

When someone fails to live up to that fantasy, we believe we can use disrespect as punishment.

Respect

Respect is the ongoing recognition of others' humanity. It directs us to look past the imperfections of others and to relate to them as equals.

Respect is much more than tolerance and acceptance, for within respect there is also a desire to listen and learn. Respect understands that everyone has something to teach us.

Respect doesn't create intimacy or love, but it prepares the ground for them. Respect thus opens the door to deeper relationships with others, ourselves, and the Divine.

Martin's Story

Martin was one of those fathers who demanded respect, and did it with a loud voice. One day, his thirteen-year-old son, Bill, yelled back, "If you want respect, then act like a father instead of a bully." With that, his son earned a slap across the face and then a couple more, just for good measure.

Bill's words cut deep, for Martin knew they were true. Martin saw that he was becoming like his own father, something he had promised himself would never happen. As truth has a tendency to do, Bill's words—and Martin's own behavior—haunted him. His wife had died of cancer, but if she hadn't, she most likely would have divorced him because of his bullying behavior.

Soon after this incident, Bill got into some trouble at school for fighting, and Martin was called in to a meeting with the school counselor to help with his son.

The counselor, with compassion in her voice, said to Martin, "Bill tells me he lost his mother and this is why he's so angry and disrespectful to everyone, and especially his teachers. Can you give us any insights on his behavior?"

Martin replied, "I believe this has little if anything to do with the death of Bill's mother. He has been disrespectful for years, and it's because of me. Truth be told, I've become a disrespectful, petty man like my father, and my son is growing up to be a mirror image of me. I'm not proud of this."

The counselor was shocked by Martin's response, but this opened up a frank and serious discussion that resulted in Martin deciding to see a family counselor with Bill. Martin also started taking Bill to services at the church down the street where Bill's mother had attended, and both enrolled in a class on better living through values.

Over the next couple of years, they developed a caring relationship based on genuine respect for each other. Martin's proudest moment was years later, when Bill asked him to stand at the altar with him at his wedding.

Questions for contemplation:

1. Is there someone (or are there multiple people) in your life whom you feel you should treat with more respect? How can you change your interactions with them in order to demonstrate that respect?

2. Who is the most respectful person you know? What specific things have you seen them do, perhaps repeatedly, that demonstrate this respectfulness? Which of these might you want to practice in your own relationships?

3. As of right now, where do you place yourself on the continuum from disrespect to respect?

Ignorance   **Awareness**

Ignorance

Ignorance is not a simple refusal to learn. It is a blindness we choose out of a fear of responsibility.

Spiritual ignorance comes from an unwillingness to accept and embrace life's mysteries and uncertainties. Instead of engaging (and often wrestling) with these challenges, we turn away from them. In making this decision, we do ourselves and others a profound disservice, for it is only in living through these challenges that we find meaning and create a moral life.

As children and adolescents, we slowly learn the ways of the world. In the process, our ignorance steadily shrinks and our knowledge grows. As adults, we are called to continue this process with an emphasis on moral and spiritual development, which can slowly lead us to wisdom. This process is never easy, it is often painful, and it never ends. When we try to ignore or avoid it, in an attempt to blunt the pain of growth, we only blunt our growth and increase our pain.

Among adults, the most common form of ignorance is looking to others—other people, institutions, codes, religions, movements, and forms of authority—to tell us what to believe and how to act. We want these authorities to make our difficult day-to-day moral decisions for us. In handing over these choices to others, however, we ignore not only our own moral responsibilities, but our own deepest call for meaning and connection.

Awareness

As a Spiritual Principle, awareness is not just the physical act of paying attention, it is being open to and appreciating what is happening around us and what is going on inside us. It is seeing the stars on a moonless night. It is hearing the joyful laughter of children playing ball down the street. It is noticing that there are more homeless people walking the street than there used to be. It is realizing that our elderly neighbor hasn't been out to pick up her newspaper all day—and then calling her to make sure she's okay.

Awareness pushes us to be awake and to fully experience the present moment. It urges us to engage with reality, despite our fears and worries and uncertainty. In awareness, we suspend judgments, at least temporarily.

Awareness is active, not passive. It is not always peaceful, for it challenges us to be fully involved with life—though, if we practice it regularly, it often leads to peace of mind.

By practicing awareness, we learn that every person, thing, situation, and moment we encounter has something to teach us, even if it's only what to avoid or be wary of. Awareness understands that truths are everywhere and available to us at all times—and that discovering or touching a truth always leads to greater humility.

Awareness allows us to see our full range of options, choices, and opportunities. It helps us to more clearly understand our weaknesses and limitations. It helps us to respond rather than merely react. And it enables us to step away from our reptilian brain, move into our neocortex, and transform the present moment into a spiritual experience.

Annabelle's Story

Annabelle worked as the human resources director at a large department store in Chicago. The Christmas season was about to begin, and she needed to make many new temporary hires.

In his interview, Bruce presented himself well. He was well dressed, polite, clever, and charming. There were a couple of gaps in his resume, but he explained them away easily. Annabelle hired him, but told herself that she needed to check up on those gaps.

Whenever Annabelle saw Bruce at work, he was polite and friendly. Each time she saw him, she reminded herself to check on those gaps. But it was the Christmas season, the busiest time of the year for almost everyone at the store. She kept letting the task slide.

One day, two detectives showed up at her office wanting to talk with Bruce. The day before, a woman had reported that a man followed her from the store. When she got to her car, he tried to push her into the back seat and assault her. Luckily, she was able to fight him off. She immediately called the police.

They checked on registered sex offenders in the area. Bruce was one of them. Annabelle's first thought was Why didn't I do that background check?

She called down to Bruce's service desk. His co-worker answered. It turned out that Bruce hadn't come to work that day. In fact, he never showed up again. The police found and arrested him three weeks later.

What shook Annabelle most was how easy it had been to allow herself to remain ignorant. Even though she had suspicions about Bruce's history, she repeatedly failed to act on them. In hiring Bruce's replacement—and all other employees henceforth—Annabelle remembered this incident and let her awareness be her guide.

Questions for contemplation:

1. Is there something in your life that you feel called to pay attention to, but have ignored or swept aside? Do you have any insights about why you are not paying attention to this issue? Can you begin attending to it now?

2. Find a safe place where you can sit comfortably—a place away from computers, televisions, and phones. For twenty to thirty minutes, simply breathe quietly and pay attention to the smells, sounds, and other sensations of the world around you. What do you discover—or rediscover—about the world or yourself from this brief period of awareness? Do you feel you can benefit from making this a spiritual practice that you do on a regular basis?

3. As of right now, where do you place yourself on the continuum from ignorance to awareness?

Envy	Appreciation

Envy

Envy is a cousin to greed. While greed has an aggressive edge, however, envy has an air of sadness and self-pity. *Poor me. Other people have what I want, but I don't get to have it.*

The heaviness of envy can pull us down, keeping us stuck in wanting without acting. But envy can sometimes create a strong desire to change, to act, to incorporate positive Spiritual Principles into our life, and to find our moral compass. This is how role models work: we observe them, admire them, envy them, want to be like them, want what they have, and ultimately choose to follow in their footsteps. In this way, envy has the potential to transform into positive spiritual action.

While greed is impersonal—we want something (or more of something), we want it badly, and no amount of it is enough—envy is personal. Envy isn't just about acquisition. Filled with envy, we look at those who already have what we crave, and we bear them ill will. When others succeed or receive blessings, instead of sharing their happiness, we feel more envy.

Envy often involves demeaning others. "What did she do to deserve it?" "Look at her in that fancy new dress. It would look so much better on me." "That car is wasted on him. He can't even begin to appreciate its fine design and engineering."

In its crudest form, envy can cause us to take pleasure in the misfortunes or pain of others—or, worst of all, it can encourage us to create misfortune or pain for them.

Appreciation

As with envy, appreciation focuses our energies outward. With appreciation, however, there is no ill will—only joy, awe, and wonder. Instead of draining our energy, appreciation builds or enhances it.

Appreciation often partners with curiosity, leading to new knowledge and learning. For example, when my wife, some friends, and I were on a vacation in Montana, we stopped at an outdoor art fair, where a woman was making glass beads using an oxy-propane torch. I stood there for more than an hour and a half, watching and asking questions. When we got home, I began investigating the art of glass bead making, and two years later I found someone to teach it to me. From my appreciation of the talents of that woman in Montana, a wonderful hobby emerged.

Appreciation enables us to focus on and learn from the talents and skills of others, the beauty and glory of nature, the wisdom of the ages, and the wonderment of human relationships. It gives us glimpses of how things fit together.

Appreciation can also help us to realize and contemplate our own potential—for part of appreciation is appreciating the skills, talents, and wisdom we have been given (while also remaining humble, of course).

Barbara's Story

Barbara knew how to appreciate people, food, and pretty much everything else. She ran a small bakery and deli, and all her employees loved her. One of her bakers described her this way:

"I would never want to work for anyone but Barbara. She never forgets a birthday and always has a kind word, even when she's telling you how you can do your job better."

When Larry, a longtime employee, had to leave the company because his wife was taking a job in another state, Barbara cried and helped the family pack. She also gave him a card that read, "Thank you for all the ways you helped make the company—and all of us—be better." And, of course, she gave Larry a big basket of bread, cheeses, and desserts for the trip to his family's new home.

Barbara had grown up poor, in a somewhat chaotic home, but she insisted that her upbringing had helped to make her strong. "My struggles as a child taught me so much. I learned the value of a dollar and how to work hard. My parents weren't always the best role models, but they always loved us and never abused us—and their mistakes and weaknesses taught me what not to do. I love both of them and am glad to be able to make life a little better for them." This was obvious every day around noon, when Barbara's parents would come by and be treated to a good lunch.

If someone invited Barbara over to their home for a simple meal, they would get a handwritten thank-you card in the mail a few days later. Going for a walk with her in the woods was an adventure in appreciation. Every few minutes, she would stop to point out some new "nature treasure," as she would call it. "Look, look here! See the fox hiding in the bushes?"

When new acquaintances asked Barbara for the source of her appreciation, she shrugged and said, "I try to see life as my Higher Power would have me see it. I have only one prayer: thank you."

Some of Barbara's employees secretly envied her, wishing they could be as appreciative and serene about life as she was. When of them confessed this to Barbara one day, Barbara nearly doubled over in a fit of laughter. Then she said, "Honey, I wasn't *born this way. I learned it and grew into it. You can do it just as well as I can. In fact, you've already started, by wanting to do it."*

Questions for contemplation:

1. Is there anyone you envy? If so, whom—and why?
   Is there anything you can do to have what they have
   or be where they are, while following positive Spiritual
   Principles? If so, can you begin to work toward that goal?
   If not, can you let go of your envy and focus your energies
   on something ethical that *can* bear fruit?

2. What three things in your life do you most appreciate?
   Why? What can you do to appreciate these things more?

3. As of right now, where do you place yourself on the
   continuum from envy to appreciation?

| Unbridled Worry | Serenity |

Unbridled Worry

Morality demands that we have faith, but unbridled worry has no faith in anything. It is partly a dark fog, partly mental noise. It mentally fast-forwards everything to its most negative potential outcome, then takes that outcome deeply seriously, no matter how unlikely it may be. In unbridled worry, there's blindness to the positive aspects of life. These are sensed and seen as setups for disappointment.

Unbridled worry combines fear with anxiety and agitation. It urges us constantly to solve problems and to prevent or avoid potential ones. Solving and avoiding problems can be helpful, of course. But because the concerns of unbridled worry are endless, we make ourselves and others unhappy and drain away everyone's spiritual energy.

Unbridled worry is like a virus. First, it tries to control us. If it succeeds, then it attempts to control others through us, creating a community of worry and agitation.

When worries or concerns come into a relationship, people naturally try to address and solve them. But because, in unbridled worry, the concerns are endless, we end up controlling conversations, controlling others, and draining away spiritual energy into a black hole of doubt.

Serenity

One of the biggest benefits of living a moral life is serenity. As we surrender ourselves to doing the next right thing, and then the next, moment after moment and day after day, serenity naturally appears in our life, healing our mind and calming our heart.

Serenity can only take place here and now, as we direct our energies toward life as it is in the present moment, seeing what is before us and doing what we are called to do.

Serenity also occurs when we are able to incorporate positive Spiritual Principles into our lives, so that their slow, steady, comforting rhythm becomes ours. Serenity is thus the result of our moral achievements.

Pauline's Story

Pauline was fourteen going on forty. She worried about everything. When a teacher handed out an assignment, Pauline's first reaction was a fear that she would do it wrong.

Her friends and family nicknamed her "What If?" When people tried to plan anything with her, she would usually come up with a barrage of "what ifs." What if it rains? What if the car gets a flat tire? What if I get the directions wrong? What if nobody there likes me?

Then one day, at a party, Pauline was doing her "what ifs" about an upcoming free concert in the park. The girl next to her laughed and said, "Chill out—smoke this." She handed Pauline a pipe. Pauline took a somewhat reluctant hit, and then another. By the end of the evening, she felt her "what ifs" change over to "whatevers."

Within a month, Pauline was smoking pot or hash every day. She loved how it settled her down and moved her "what ifs" and worries into a separate universe.

A year later, Pauline was on the verge of failing tenth grade and being thrown out of her parents' home. One spring night, she broke down sobbing at the dinner table and asked her parents to enroll her in a drug treatment program. They agreed, and she began treatment two weeks later.

Pauline liked the program and most of the people in it. Breaking her marijuana habit was difficult, yet doable. But her worries began multiplying again, yammering at her and making her anxious and tense.

Pauline's treatment counselor told her that when she started to go to self-help meetings, she needed to find the calmest woman there to be her sponsor. This was how Pauline met Belle.

Over the next two years, Belle taught Pauline how to let go, how to take things easy, how to work the Serenity Prayer, and how to have faith—first in the Twelve Step program, next in Belle, and, finally, in herself. Belle and Pauline put together three short prayers that Pauline would say when worries started to form in her head. She also learned to find activities to channel her energies; this helped her get her GED and then enroll in college.

Over time, Pauline developed a sense of serenity that didn't come from a pipe or a joint, but from a life centered on positive Spiritual Principles.

Questions for contemplation:

1. What are the things that worry you most—or that, when you worry about them, most tempt you to fall into despair? How do these worries get in your way? How do they help you? Are you willing to let these worries go? How would your life be different if you did let them go?

2. When in your life have you experienced the most serenity? Why? What can you do to create some of those same conditions in your life now? Can you think of five things you can do to add more serenity to your life?

3. As of right now, where do you place yourself on the continuum from unbridled worry to serenity?

| Injustice | Justice |

Injustice

Injustice is active and intentional. It is the deliberate damaging of the rights of others for our own imagined benefit.

When we become unjust, our hearts turn cold, but our minds may become cunning. It's a dangerous mix.

Ultimately, every act of injustice harms both its intended victim and the person who acts unjustly. It is a classic lose-lose arrangement.

Justice

Life will never be completely (or even mostly) just. It never has been and never will be, which is precisely why we need to practice and seek justice as much as we can, and as best we can.

Justice is created. It is a goal, an intention, and an achievement. When wrongs get made right and when positive Spiritual Principles are placed ahead of instinct and personality, justice is produced, one human action at a time.

Justice seeks to counter wrongdoing, heal wounds, and restore spiritual harmony and balance. We do this by admitting our mistakes, apologizing, making amends, and doing the next right thing.

We also help create justice when we allow those who have harmed us to admit their own mistakes and make appropriate amends.

Justice often involves holding others accountable for their actions and decisions, but without our succumbing to the temptation of judgmentalism or apathy. It also means holding ourselves accountable for our actions and decisions in precisely the same way.

Justice is often the first step toward healing. Sometimes a single act of justice is all that is needed to begin healing old wounds. My client Nancy told me, "I remember the day my attacker stood in court and that one word, *guilty*, was read. His head hung low, and that's when I started to raise mine. My community stood with me as the jury and the judge said that what he had done to me was wrong, and that he would be held accountable. That was when my suffering started to be transformed. I'll never forget the faces of those men and women on the jury. To me they will always be the faces of justice."

Nelson's Story

For more than fifteen years, Nelson woke up at four every weekday morning in order to be at work by six. He worked until three, and then went to his second job, where he worked until nine. This was his life during the week. On Saturdays, he usually would do volunteer work, and on Sundays, he would relax, go to church, or visit with friends.

Nelson lived very simply, in a small apartment. He was a good neighbor, and almost everyone who met him liked him. Some people wondered, though, what he did with much of the money he made at his two jobs.

For those fifteen-plus years, Nelson used most of his earnings to help a mother and her two daughters live good lives. He provided them with most of their financial support, and helped put both daughters through college. Eventually, one became a nurse and the other became an engineer.

During those fifteen-plus years, Nelson met this family only three times. He attended each daughter's college graduation, to which he was invited. The other time had been more than fifteen years earlier, at the funeral of the girls' father, Riaz.

The day Nelson had graduated from college, he and his friends celebrated late into the night. At 1:00 a.m., Nelson stopped drinking beer and switched to coffee. Around 3:30, when he felt reasonably sober, he got in his car and drove home through a torrential downpour, singing at the top of his lungs along with Aretha Franklin, whose music was cranked up on his car stereo. As he steered around a corner, he didn't see Riaz stepping off the curb. His car plowed directly into Riaz.

Nelson called the police from the scene of the accident. An ambulance and police car soon arrived, but Riaz died in the hospital the following day.

Nelson was never charged with a crime. But he knew that if he hadn't been drinking, hadn't been singing so loudly, and had been more careful and observant—which he should have been in such a big storm—then Riaz would not have died.

Nelson saw it as his duty to provide for Riaz's family just as Riaz would have provided for them. He sought to do restitution to the innocent family. By his own standards of justice, he'd wronged the family, but he hadn't had the courage to face justice himself.

When Nelson was forty-one, he was diagnosed with pancreatic cancer, which progressed rapidly. Two months later, he had to stop working; four months later, he was placed in hospice care.

One day, as he lay in bed reading, the three women came to his bedside. "We've been talking," the mother said, "and we've decided that if you're willing, we'd like to help care for you during your remaining days. We know that you worked so hard to right

the wrong you did that you never had a family of your own. We
want to be your family during your remaining days. We ask only
one thing: that you forgive yourself, as we did years ago."

Questions for contemplation:

1. Think of two recent situations in which you feel you
   acted unjustly. What were the consequences for other
   people in each case? What were the consequences for
   you? In each case, what can you do now, or in the near
   future, to make amends and create justice?

2. What three specific, practical, concrete things can you
   do—day by day and moment by moment—to help create
   more justice in the world?

3. As of right now, where do you place yourself on the
   continuum from injustice to justice?

EPILOGUE

EMBRACING YOUR MORAL DEVELOPMENT

Most children, many adolescents, and even some adults live in *moral innocence*. It's a state in which we lack clarity about the world and about ourselves as human beings. We may also deny or minimize our own dark sides—our own attraction to and fascination with negative spiritual principles.

In a state of moral innocence, we see the world in simple ways. As moral innocents, we seek new and pleasurable sensations and experiences, usually with little or no thought about their consequences, either for ourselves or others. We feel little or no guilt, and we may even feel a bit self-righteous.

This innocence can become a danger to us, and our self-righteousness can become a danger to others, especially as we grow older. We may tilt at the windmills of causes or positions just for the excitement and attention that adopting such causes can bring. Yet we may refuse to accept (or try to avoid) any accountability and responsibility for our actions. We may also be blind to the outcomes and consequences of those actions. We may thus easily—and sometimes unwittingly—do harm to others. As Rollo May observed in his book *Power and Innocence: A Search for the Sources of Violence,* "Innocence as a shield from responsibility is also a shield from growth." Innocence that refuses to see its own evilness is no longer innocent: it's evil.

In such cases, we have not yet eaten from the tree of spiritual knowledge, as we all must if we want to grow spiritually. But usually life and its suffering, crises, and tragedies eventually overtake us; they cannot be escaped by our trying to stay innocent. Maturity means letting go of our innocence, even when that means feeling confusion and pain.

For the great majority of us, life relieves us of our innocence as we get older. The next step in our moral development is typically *moralism*, a moral framework characterized by black-and-white, right-and-wrong thinking that reflects a need for power and control. This is a stage that most healthy adults move through, but it is still a self-centered, spiritually immature stage and not a destination.

Sadly, however, many people and groups get seduced into believing that moralism is the end point. Instead of practicing and living by positive Spiritual Principles, moralists hide behind shallow imitations of these principles. They believe they have a monopoly on interpreting these Principles, and that their job is to show others how and why they are wrong.

Behind their stated desire to do the right thing, people trapped in moralism confuse their own self-righteous ideas with positive Spiritual Principles, and typically interpret those Principles in ways that serve their egos and a primitive need for security rather than humanity.

Moralism often declares, "You are either with us or against us." It finds or creates villains onto which it projects its own attraction to negative spiritual principles. It turns its back on questioning, critical thinking, uncertainty, and ambiguity, and insists that it already has all the answers. It is always ready to teach but has no interest in learning. Moralism thus lacks the humility needed to be just.

Spiritual maturity means that we must grow out of moralism and into a more *authentic morality*. We may have moments or periods in which we drift or run back into the false security that moralism appears to offer, but eventually, we choose spiritual growth over self-deception. Paradoxically, this spiritual growth involves becoming ever more aware of our own flaws, limitations, and incompleteness.

Authentic morality accepts that while right and wrong can sometimes be clearly defined, much of the time we must wrestle with different perspectives and ideas in order to do the next right thing. Authentic morality works to be inclusive. It does not know where it will discover more wisdom and deeper truths, but it knows that if it stays open, answers will come. It seeks to heal wounds rather than to create them, and it is regularly humbled by its own incompleteness.

Authentic morality values questions, uncertainty, and the process of discovery. It understands negative spiritual principles and how they can seduce us, especially during times of fear and times of abundance. And it enables us to feel awe and joy in our practical, day-to-day expression of positive Spiritual Principles.

This book is an invitation to find, use, and appreciate your own moral compass.

APPENDICES

The worksheets contained in these appendices may be photocopied for personal use.

POSITIVE SPIRITUAL PRINCIPLES

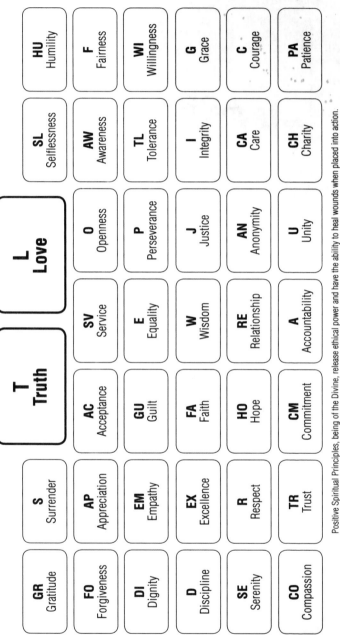

GR Gratitude	**S** Surrender	**T** Truth	**L** Love	**SL** Selflessness	**HU** Humility
FO Forgiveness	**AP** Appreciation	**AC** Acceptance	**SV** Service	**AW** Awareness	**F** Fairness
DI Dignity	**EM** Empathy	**GU** Guilt	**E** Equality	**O** Openness	**WI** Willingness
D Discipline	**EX** Excellence	**FA** Faith	**W** Wisdom	**P** Perseverance	**I** Integrity	**TL** Tolerance	**G** Grace
SE Serenity	**R** Respect	**HO** Hope	**RE** Relationship	**J** Justice	**CA** Care	**C** Courage
CO Compassion	**TR** Trust	**CM** Commitment	**A** Accountability	**AN** Anonymity	**CH** Charity
			U Unity	**PA** Patience

Positive Spiritual Principles, being of the Divine, release ethical power and have the ability to heal wounds when placed into action. It is in how we bring them together that our value system gets created.

NEGATIVE SPIRITUAL PRINCIPLES

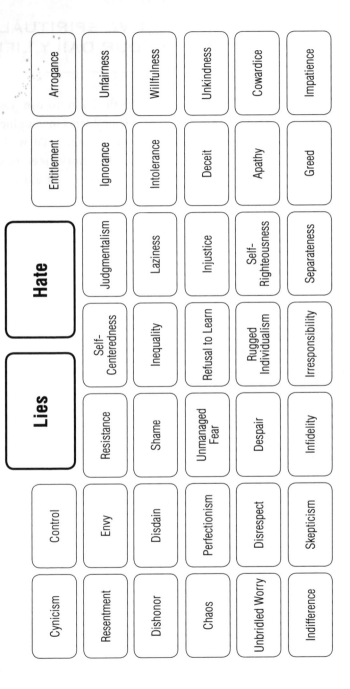

	Lies		**Hate**			
Cynicism	Control	Self-Centeredness	Judgmentalism	Entitlement	Arrogance
Resentment	Envy	Resistance	Inequality	Laziness	Ignorance	Unfairness
Dishonor	Disdain	Shame	Refusal to Learn	Injustice	Intolerance	Willfulness
Chaos	Perfectionism	Unmanaged Fear	Rugged Individualism	Self-Righteousness	Deceit	Unkindness
Unbridled Worry	Disrespect	Despair	Irresponsibility	Separateness	Apathy	Cowardice
Indifference	Skepticism	Infidelity		Greed	Impatience

APPLYING POSITIVE SPIRITUAL PRINCIPLES IN YOUR DAILY LIFE

In this section, I'll give you a practical way to use positive Spiritual Principles to solve specific problems in your life.

This involves applying a simple formula. I'll walk you through an example and then provide a worksheet for using the formula in your own situation. (Feel free to photocopy this worksheet and use it over and over.)

Step 1

Think of a problem you are dealing with or that has been troubling you. Examples:

- I have a lot of resentment toward my spouse.

- I feel bad about the way I treat my children.

- I stole money from my brother and his family. I want to tell them and pay it back.

- I'm close to flunking out of school.

- I gave up a child fifteen years ago and have never talked to anyone about it.

Sample problem: I've been stealing money from my brother and his family for the last year. When I've gone over to their house, I've gone through his wife's purse and the drawers where they keep money. I've also gone through his wallet at times. Each time I've taken between $50 and $100. Over the year, it's added up to about $3,000.

Step 2

From the Positive Spiritual Principles chart in Appendix A, pick the top five Principles you believe you will need to solve this problem. The specific problem will define the Principles you need. (As you use this chart over time, you will see how different problems call for different Principles.)

Sample principles: Fairness (F), Willingness (WI), Awareness (AW), Courage (C), Acceptance (AC)

Step 3

Now prioritize these five positive Spiritual Principles, from most important or necessary to least, based on your own best judgment. This will give you your customized formula for solving this specific problem.

Sample prioritization: Willingness (WI), Courage (C), Fairness (F), Awareness (AW), Acceptance (AC)

Sample formula: WI + C + F + AW + AC

Step 4

Turn these Principles into actions. Remember, positive Spiritual Principles need to become actions in order to release their healing and problem-solving properties. So, create a list of specific actions you will take that make use of each Principle. Include times or deadlines as appropriate.

You may want to assign more actions to the Principles with higher priorities. For example, for the most important Principle, create a list of five actions; for the second most important, create a list of four actions; for the third most important, create a list of three actions; and so on. Your list of specific, concrete actions will look something like this:

Sample actions from your formula:

WI (five actions)

1. I will write down all the reasons why I want to tell my brother about the stealing. I will do this today.

2. I will talk with a friend, my clergyperson, or my recovery sponsor about what I've done and why I want to heal this wound. I will do this within a week.

3. I will find a counselor and make an appointment to start dealing with the reasons I have acted in this way.

4. I will call my sister-in-law and set up a date to go tell her.

5. I will practice telling my brother the truth about what I did to him and his family and offering to make amends.

C (four actions)

1. I will talk with a friend, my clergyperson, or my recovery sponsor about what I've done and why I want to heal this wound. *(Notice that some actions, such as this one, work for multiple Principles.)*

2. I will talk to three people I trust about what courage is and how they muster it when they need it.

3. I will meet with my brother, tell him what I did, apologize, offer to make amends, and make my first repayment.

4. I will ask my Higher Power daily for the courage to tell my brother, apologize, and make amends.

F (three actions)

1. I will make a list of every time I can remember stealing from my brother and his wife, and the amount I took each time. I will then add 10 percent for times I may not have remembered.

2. When I meet with my brother, I will ask him what he needs from me to set this straight.

3. I will sign up for and do one hundred hours of volunteer work at the local homeless shelter.

AW (two actions)

1. I will find a counselor and make an appointment to start dealing with the reasons I have acted in this way. *(This also appears under Willingness.)*

2. I will write a paragraph or two about the type of person I want to be going forward. I will read this every day until I've talked with and fully repaid my brother.

AC (one action)

1. I will write out a list of all the ways this could go bad, such as my brother never wanting to talk to me again, or not wanting me to be alone in his home again, or having me arrested. I will accept that any of these things—or other, worse things I haven't imagined—may happen, and that whatever happens, it will be because of what I did.

Step 5

Put your solution into motion by doing *everything* on your lists within the time you have agreed to do them.

APPLYING POSITIVE SPIRITUAL PRINCIPLES WORKSHEET

Step 1: Think of a problem you are dealing with or that has been troubling you:

_____

_____

_____

_____

Step 2: From the Positive Spiritual Principles chart in Appendix A, pick the top five Principles you believe you will need to solve this problem:

_____

_____

_____

_____

_____

Step 3: Prioritize these five positive Spiritual Principles, from most important to least important:

_____

_____

_____

_____

_____

Step 4: Create a list of specific actions you will take that make use of each Principle. Include times or deadlines as appropriate. You may want to assign more actions to the principles with higher priorities:

Principle _____

Tasks that put this into action: _____

_____

Principle _____

Tasks that put this into action: _____

_____

Principle _____

Tasks that put this into action: _____

_____

Principle _____

Tasks that put this into action: _____

_____

Principle _____

Tasks that put this into action: _____

_____

Step 5: Put your solution into motion by doing *everything* on your lists within the time you have agreed to do them.

USING POSITIVE SPIRITUAL PRINCIPLES TO HELP WITH ANGER

Anger is a powerful and provocative emotion, but it is almost always a secondary emotion, a response to another painful feeling.

The biological function of anger is to enable us to protect and defend ourselves or others. Anger is instinctual, and it's the quickest and most direct route to our reptilian brain. Because the reptilian brain is the part of us that doesn't see a need for loving relationships, unmanaged anger can destroy such relationships. In most cases, three other painful emotions lie beneath anger: fear, sadness, and a sense of powerlessness. Anger is the transformation of one or more of these into a defensive, distorted reaction. To correct the distortions and manage our anger, we need to look beneath it until we can see the underlying fear, sadness, and/or powerlessness. *This means that to become better at dealing with anger, we have to become better at dealing with fear, sadness, and things we feel powerless over.*

Now look at the Sample Anger Worksheet on the next page. Here, several anger-related situations are listed, together with some other details. Make a copy (or several) of the blank worksheet on page 238, then think of five situations in which you got angry and list them in the first column. Remembering that anger is a secondary emotion, reflect on each event and determine what was under the anger: fear, sadness, a sense of powerlessness, or some combination of them. Then check the appropriate box(es). Now go to the Positive Spiritual Principles chart in Appendix A. Review the forty-one positive Principles and pick the two or three that you feel can best help you handle this situation.

SAMPLE
Anger Worksheet: Applying Positive Spiritual Principles

List situations in which you have become angry.	Which of these emotions are/were present? Check all that apply.			Which positive Spiritual Principle(s) can help you solve this issue?
	FEAR	SADNESS	POWER-LESSNESS	
EXAMPLE: Somebody cut me off on the freeway.	☒	☐	☐	• Tolerance • Patience
EXAMPLE: My boss told us that our health care premiums will be going up.	☐	☐	☒	• Acceptance • Fairness • Discipline
EXAMPLE: My mother has been diagnosed with cancer.	☐	☒	☐	• Compassion • Hope • Gratitude
	☐	☐	☐	
	☐	☐	☐	

Anger Worksheet: Applying Positive Spiritual Principles

List situations in which you have become angry.	Which of these emotions are/were present? Check all that apply.			Which positive Spiritual Principle(s) can help you solve this issue?
	FEAR	SADNESS	POWER-LESSNESS	
	☐	☐	☐	
	☐	☐	☐	
	☐	☐	☐	
	☐	☐	☐	
	☐	☐	☐	

DIRECTING OUR ENERGIES TOWARD POSITIVE SPIRITUAL PRINCIPLES THROUGH LANGUAGE

Because we use language to direct our energies, what we say to ourselves and others is vastly important. In particular, we can use language to positively influence ourselves by directing our energies to the spiritual and thinking (rather than the instinctual and reactive) parts of our brain.

I often ask my clients, "How are you using your internal language? Does it help you stay focused, and set and reach goals, or do your mental conversations easily push you off track?" We then start to talk about "gate language."

Just as we have gates called heart valves that regulate the flow of blood into and out of our hearts, language can act as a gate, directing and influencing our energies.

As a counselor, I've long been interested in why some people reach their goals and others do not. I've learned that sometimes people drain away much of their own positive internal energies through the way they talk to themselves and others.

Typically, we start with good intentions and apply our energies toward reaching our goals. After we experience some setbacks or resistance, however, we may start to use language to direct our energies *away* from our goals and toward defensive positions. We end up in what I call "Victim Land" or "Tough Land." This frustrated talk causes us to lose our focus and momentum.

Victim Land is tied to our drive for pleasure. This is the domain of avoidance, where energies get used to build a case for why we can't reach our goals, or why others won't support us or allow us to succeed. Victim Land language has a whining, pleading tone, and its core message is *Don't hold me responsible.*

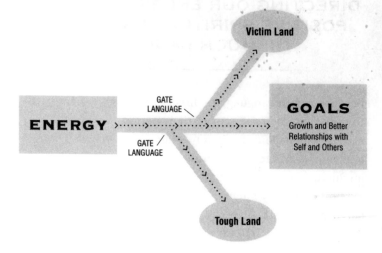

Tough Land is tied to our drive for power. This is the domain of control, where energies get redirected toward staying in control instead of reaching our goals. Tough Land language has a rough, angry, aggressive, rugged-individualist edge. It pushes others away or tries to exert power over them. Its core message is *I don't need your or anyone's help.*

Each of these forms of talk opens an internal gate that redirects our energies and thoughts toward defenses instead of goals and solutions. As a counselor, I can often hear the sound of one of these gates swinging open. I see my clients' attitudes and actions start to change, and I know that if this gate doesn't get shut, they will experience failure instead of success. My job as their counselor isn't to close these gates, but to teach them how to listen to their own words, both internal and external; to recognize when one of these gates has opened; and to change their language so that it supports them in reaching their goals.

Here are some common examples of gate language from both Victim Land and Tough Land:

Victim Land Phrases	Tough Land Phrases
I'm so tired.	I don't care what happens!
Life is not fair; life is cruel.	If people would do what I say, there wouldn't be a problem.
Why should I? No one really cares if things will work out for me.	No one else really gives a damn.
Why don't you listen to me?	Why don't you listen to me?
I've tried that, and other things, too, and nothing ever changes for the better.	Those damn liberals/conservatives/bosses/employees/elected officials! They're all a bunch of thieves and crooks, just out for themselves.
Why bother? Nothing ever happens the way I want it to.	Just leave me alone! I can take care of myself!
I want to succeed or change, but people won't let me.	I've always been on my own and always will be.
If you had my life, you would understand why I can't do that.	All that counts is power and money. I'm gonna make sure I get mine.
I already know it won't work.	I'm so damn stupid.

As you've probably noticed, some of the phrases in Victim Land and Tough Land are similar or identical. Sometimes, our tone and attitude are what determine whether our energy gets diverted into Victim Land or Tough Land. For example, if said with self-pity, *Why don't you listen to me?* can open the gate to Victim Land. But if it's said with anger and an edge, then the gate to Tough Land opens. Either way, however, our energy is diverted away from achievement and growth and toward defenses and failure.

EXERCISES

Which "land" are you tempted to travel to most often?

_____

Now, notice the gate language you most often use to put yourself in these places.

What are the five most common phrases or statements you use to move yourself into Tough Land?

1._____

2._____

3._____

4._____

5._____

What are the five most common phrases or statements you use to move yourself into Victim Land?

1._____

2._____

3._____

4._____

5._____

Now, write a phrase or statement that counters your Tough Land and Victim Land entries with a positive message that moves you away from defensiveness and failure toward achievement and growth:

_____

_____

ABOUT THE AUTHOR

CRAIG M. NAKKEN, MSW, LCSW, LMFT is a family therapist, author, international lecturer, and trainer who specializes in recovery from addictions. Craig began his counseling career in 1972 at Pharm House in Minneapolis, where he worked with addicts who came in off the street. He served as Pharm House's director of outpatient treatment services from 1975 to 1977.

Craig was a senior counselor at Family Renewal Center in Minneapolis from 1977 to 1983, then a counselor in private practice until 1986, when he joined the Family Therapy Institute in St. Paul. Craig served as vice president at Family Therapy Institute until 1994. Since 1995, he has been in private practice in St. Paul.

Craig received his master's degree in social work from the University of Minnesota in 1985. He has trained counselors as an instructor at the Florida State Summer School on Addiction in Jacksonville, Florida (1989–2005), and at the Rutgers Summer School of Alcohol Studies in New Brunswick, New Jersey (1986–present).

Craig shares his knowledge and his message of hope in his books and talks. His first book, *The Addictive Personality: Roots, Rituals & Recovery*, was published in 1988 and is now in its second edition, with more than 500,000 copies in print. In 2000, Craig authored *Reclaim Your Family from Addiction: How Couples and Families Recover Love and Meaning*, a book and a set of workbooks that help families recover from the illness of addiction.

Craig has also created two DVDs, *Reclaim Your Family from Addiction* and *A Social Worker's Perspective on the Twelve Steps*, as well as workbooks for couples and families to help them in their healing. (All of these are available through Hazelden Foundation at hazelden.org.)

Craig's teaching and training have taken him to Norway, China, Denmark, Greece, Sweden, Australia, Iceland, Singapore, Mexico, Puerto Rico, Panama, and Russia, as well as across the United States. He presented at the first-ever Conference on Addictions in Beijing, China, in 2002; at the All Asian Conference on Addictions in Singapore in 2004; and at the World Forum Against Drugs in Stockholm, Sweden, in 2008.

Hazelden, a national nonprofit organization founded in 1949, helps people reclaim their lives from the disease of addiction. Built on decades of knowledge and experience, Hazelden offers a comprehensive approach to addiction that addresses the full range of patient, family, and professional needs, including treatment and continuing care for youth and adults, research, higher learning, public education and advocacy, and publishing.

A life of recovery is lived "one day at a time." Hazelden publications, both educational and inspirational, support and strengthen lifelong recovery. In 1954, Hazelden published *Twenty-Four Hours a Day*, the first daily meditation book for recovering alcoholics, and Hazelden continues to publish works to inspire and guide individuals in treatment and recovery, and their loved ones. Professionals who work to prevent and treat addiction also turn to Hazelden for evidence-based curricula, informational materials, and videos for use in schools, treatment programs, and correctional programs.

Through published works, Hazelden extends the reach of hope, encouragement, help, and support to individuals, families, and communities affected by addiction and related issues.

For questions about Hazelden publications,
please call 800-328-9000
or visit us online at hazelden.org/bookstore.